Praise for

In my capacit… g Rare Incidence Syndromes (TRIS) project, I continually look for resources for parents beginning the journey into the rare trisomy world. There is so much to learn and so many decisions to make. Beverly Jacobson's book, *From Diagnosis to Delivery*, provides a needed collection of facts, anecdotes and recommendations. Whatever the outcome, the information will assist parents-to-be and others involved in the arrival of a newborn with trisomy 18 [or any prenatal diagnosis] a positive perspective and concrete steps for the initial journey.

Deborah A. Bruns, Ph.D.
Lead researcher, Tracking Rare Incidence Syndromes (TRIS) project
Professor, Special Education program
School of Education, Southern Illinois University Carbondale

As a surgeon, I'm trained to thoroughly review medical literature and provide realistic expectations to my patients regarding their diagnoses and treatment options. As a Christian and a mother, my heart leads me to encourage and provide hope to my patients as much as possible. When I received the presumptive diagnosis of Trisomy 18 for our precious baby boy Asher, a son I've been wanting to have all my life, no training could have prepared me for the roller coaster ride of emotions that we were forced to go on. Life is hard, medicine is not always exact, most doctors do care, but we are human and when we don't have answers, we can lose our way. Of all the tools I had in my arsenal to deal with such a devastating diagnosis (and ultimately a loss), it was my faith that help me through, and it is my faith that continues to carry me.

As I read through the pages of Beverly Jacobson's *From Diagnosis to Delivery*, I felt her words healing wounds in me that I didn't think could ever heal. This book reminded me that we are all beautifully and wonderfully made, that we don't have all the answers (nor do we need to), that we are and always will be mothers who love our children, in life and in death, in spite of any diagnosis, and regardless of the outcome. *From Diagnosis to Delivery* is a vital book for information, for hope, and for healing.

Courtney E. Gibson, M.D., F.A.C.S.
Assistant Professor of Surgery
Yale-New Haven Hospital/Yale University School of Medicine

From Diagnosis to Delivery is a roadmap for parents who have received a life-limiting diagnosis for their unborn child. Beverly's candid and often raw account of her own journey offers the reader hope and a life-line. This book outlines, in detail, any possible scenario parents of an unborn special-needs child may face with diplomacy and dignity. If you have just one book in your tool belt, this is the one to have!

Mellisa Blackburn
Executive Director, Yellow Horse Media

This book is a result of the author's driving force to advocate for trisomy families. She clearly references the tragic reality that discrimination against babies with a life-limiting diagnosis is all too real. Partly due to bias, partly due to ignorance, the push to abort is real. Powerfully written, this book will arm you with practical ideas. You will appreciate how she lays out foundational truths, truths that will center you and empower you while dealing with this unprecedented life event. Knowledge is power.

Janet Vickrey RN, BSN

From Diagnosis to Delivery is a compassionate, accessible, invaluable tool in the hands of parents who are facing a life-limiting diagnosis for their unborn child. Beverly's own journey through the diagnosis of Trisomy 18 for her daughter Verity gives her a unique perspective into the heartache, challenges, grief, and joy surrounding the pregnancy, delivery, and often, but not always, loss of these rare and beautiful children. Beverly gently encourages advocacy for parents who need to have their voices heard as they navigate the pregnancy with a child they are often told is "incompatible with life." *From Diagnosis to Delivery* helps parents navigate everything from initial diagnosis, finding a medical team that supports the wishes of the parent, advocacy after delivery, facing loss, and providing for a medically fragile child. Beverly writes in a conversational tone, putting invaluable information and tools into the hands of the parents who love their children unconditionally.

Joyce Zick
TEAM Missionary to Italy
Member of Verity's Village Board of Directors

FROM DIAGNOSIS TO DELIVERY

What to Expect When the Unexpected Happens During Your Pregnancy

BEVERLY JACOBSON

FROM DIAGNOSIS TO DELIVERY: What to Expect When the Unexpected Happens During Your Pregnancy.

Published by Verity's Village Press
P.O. Box 123
Monument, CO 80132

Front cover image by Rudy and Peter Skitterians from Pixabay
Author photo: Melissa Pennington

Printed in the United States of America
ISBN: 978-1-64775-400-6
Library of Congress Control Number: 2021914259

All websites listed herein are accurate at the time of publication but may change in the future or cease to exist. The listing of website references and resources does not imply endorsement of the site's entire contents. Groups and organizations are listed for informational purposes, and listing does not imply author or publisher endorsement of their activities.

Dedicated to my beautiful daughter

Verity Irene

who brings joy, love, and hope to so many people around the world simply by existing.

What a precious gift you are!

Oh, Lord...
You formed Verity's inward parts;
you knitted her together in my womb.
I praise you, for she is fearfully and wonderfully made.
Wonderful are your works;
my soul knows it very well....
Your eyes saw Verity's unformed substance;
in your book were written, every one of them,
the days that were formed for her,
when as yet there was none of them.

–Prayer based on Psalm 139:13, 14, 16

CONTENTS

Author's Notes 9

Foreword 10

SECTION 1—INTRODUCTION

Chapter 1: When the Unexpected Happens 15

Chapter 2: Where Do You Go From Here? 21
*Acceptance * Awareness * Advocacy*

Chapter 3: What Are We Looking For? 27
*Alignment * Assurance * Significance*

SECTION 2—CENTER YOURSELF (Acceptance)

Chapter 4: Finding a Firm Foundation 35
*Sarah's testimony * Centered on a foundation of truth*

Chapter 5: Dealing with Emotions 40
*Denial * Guilt * Anger * Isolation * Fear * Grief * Processing emotions * Gratitude*

Chapter 6: Living with Uncertainty 50
*Uncertainty is an unavoidable part of life * Uncertainty is a normal part of life * We choose how we meet with uncertainty * Uncertainty does not equate to helplessness * Uncertainty is exhausting * Uncertainty is part of a meaningful life*

Chapter 7: Unpacking Preconceived Ideas 56
*Preconceived ideas of the medical world * Preconceived ideas of family and friends * Preconceived ideas of your own*

SECTION 3—EDUCATE YOURSELF (Awareness)

Chapter 8: What Does Current Research Say? 67
*Know what you're looking for * Make sure the information is up-to-date * Find multiple sources * Find objective sources * Keep the big picture in mind*

Chapter 9: What If… 73
*What if the diagnosis is wrong? * What if a prenatal diagnosis is actually a drawback? * What if the diagnosis is worse than reality? * What if reality is worse than the diagnosis? * What if...*

Chapter 10: What Does Your Medical Team Say? 84
*Location matters * Take someone along with you to your appointments * Know what level of care you want for your baby * What types of interventions are you comfortable with providing? * It's all right to change your mind! * Mary's story * Suggested questions to ask your medical team*

Chapter 11: What Do Real People Say? 97
*Find your tribe * Listen and learn with discernment * Don't be afraid to reach out * Learn from as many other parents as possible * Receiving the diagnosis * Changing perspective * Family dynamics: marriage * Family dynamics: siblings * Interventions * Getting on the same page with the medical team * Different outcomes than expected * Life with a child who has special needs*

Chapter 12: What Do YOU Say? 111
*Other types of input * Fine-tuning your view of life * Overcoming "Analysis Paralysis" * Ancient words of wisdom*

SECTION 4—PREPARE YOURSELF (Advocacy)

Chapter 13: Enjoying Your Pregnancy 119
Ideas for making memories during the pregnancy

CONTENTS

(Continued)

Chapter 14: What About a Baby Shower? 123
*Before or after birth? * A practical solution * Gift ideas * Meal delivery*

Chapter 15: Preparing for Loss 128
*Preparing your other children * Ideas for making memories after delivery * Cuddle Cots * The logistics of loss * Planning a service * Cremation or casket? * Words of wisdom from parents whose children have passed*

Chapter 16: Preparing for Life 143
*Fair care * Insurance and financial considerations * Early intervention services * Specialty care providers * Home health care * Respite programs/providers * Paid parent programs * Supplemental Security Income (SSI) * Medical equipment * Home considerations and modifications * Family dynamics*

Chapter 17: Preparing Your Birth Plan 158
*Diagnosis and parental understanding thereof * Labor and delivery * Approved attendees * After-birth activities * If Baby is stillborn * A sample birth plan*

CONCLUSION

Chapter 18: From Diagnosis to Delivery…and Beyond 167

Appendix A: My Foundation of Faith 171

Appendix B: Of Healing and Miracles 175

Notes 179

Acknowledgments 183

AUTHOR'S NOTES

Quotations

Unless otherwise noted by a title, all quotations in this book are from parents who have walked this journey before you. Not all of them knew about their child's diagnosis prior to birth, but all of them are living beyond the diagnosis.

☙❧

Disclaimer

While much of the content in this book revolves around the medical world, none of the material is in any way intended to diagnose, treat, or prescribe. You should direct any relevant questions to your own doctor and medical team members. We do encourage independent research and multiple opinions, but please do not take anything from this book as the final word on your baby's condition.

☙❧

Perspective

This book is a labor of love born of my personal experiences and connections. Because of the sensitive nature of the topics in this book, it is impossible for me to stay completely objective, though I have strived to do so. While my spiritual beliefs are central to who I am and how I have perceived our journey, I am confident you will find great value in this book regardless of whether our personal beliefs align.

FOREWORD

I recently met Verity, the inspiration for this book. She had just returned from a road trip with her family and was nothing short of a firecracker! Verity was working on floor exercises with a nurse as her brother—one of eight older siblings—was quietly engaged reading a book on the couch next to his little sister. Her incredible mother, Beverly Jacobson, told Verity that I came by to meet her. But like many young children, especially when they are tired and grumpy, she couldn't be bothered interrupting her routine to acknowledge this stranger standing over her space. Beverly and I both laughed at the tenacity of this spunky little girl.

As humans, we learn to communicate with body language and words from infanthood, but a child with Trisomy 18 depends on the love of family and caretakers to address basic needs. Little Verity's loving family physically, emotionally and spiritually lifts her up, reminding her with their faith in action that our confidence is in Christ. I'm not sure if Verity can verbalize her feelings with words, but I know her family understands how to take care of her and make her an integral part of their close-knit tribe.

Beverly shared with me that her youngest daughter was so glad to be home after a family road trip. Verity recognized the familiar setting as soon as the family came through the door, and any stress from the unfamiliar settings during the vacation seemed to dissipate. When you walk in the Jacobsons' home, what you first see to your immediate left is Verity's room. It is a room any little girl would cherish, decorated in pink, with toys and books and a beautiful crib. Yet upon closer look, you recognize that there are many medical devices normally found in a hospital. This family is all-in with Verity! The Jacobsons' home is filled with more love and authenticity than I've ever witnessed.

From Diagnosis to Delivery is focused on the precious gift of every single child, whether that baby is in the womb or whether delivered into this world to live a day, a year, or 100 years. Beverly reminds the reader that even the baby that miscarries, or is stillborn, is also precious. (I was on a flight from Dallas, TX, to Orange County, CA, when I read the section about the cuddle cots, and I openly wept.)

Admittedly, I was unfamiliar with Trisomy 18 before I met Beverly at the Pro-life Innovators Summit hosted by our organization in early 2021. This mother of nine impressed our panel with her confident delivery of a very difficult topic and a professionalism often seen only in executive boardrooms. We tried to hold back tears as Beverly walked us through her pregnancy and the moment she and her husband learned of their baby's diagnosis. Her bravery, joy, and genuine love for Verity is evident. Her desire to use what she learned from her daughter's diagnosis to help other parents is a true selfless act of generosity.

Beverly openly shares the deepest feelings she experienced during her pregnancy, thoughts that many mothers would be scared to admit:

- Feeling as terrified of her baby living as she was of her dying
- Wondering how would she raise a special-needs child
- The shame of feeling her faith was weak
- Feeling completely overwhelmed and ill-equipped

Her honesty about the "what ifs" and the lack of knowledge and research related to these rare in-utero diagnoses would cause anyone to question what to do. Yet Beverly is using her experiences to help you and other parents and through her group and this book is building a steadfast community to love and support each other. She is providing hope when it is needed most.

Ten years ago, when I sat by my husband who was on life support following an AVM rupture, I read Romans 5:2-5 over and over in the hospital:

"...through whom also we have access by faith into this grace in which we stand, and rejoice in hope of the glory of God. And not only that, but we also glory in tribulations, knowing that tribulation produces perseverance; and perseverance, character, and character, hope. Now hope does not disappoint, because the love of God has been poured out in our hearts by the Holy Spirit who was given to us."

The hope I felt in the ICU, even as my husband passed away, reminded me that God is always in control. Even when—especially when—our hearts are broken. Tribulations are part of this earthly life, as you, reader, know all too well, but the love of God gives us hope.

I wasn't able to have children of my own. I can't imagine what you strong, brave mothers and fathers are feeling, or what you will take away from this book. But God intersected my life with Beverly's life, and I now understand what specifically to pray for when I learn of a Trisomy or other rare diagnosis.

As you read this book, you may wonder over and over again why God has chosen *you* to carry a baby with unique, special needs. I cannot answer that question for you, but I can tell you that our Almighty Creator sees you as a capable, brave and strong parent, someone who can absolutely do this!

I thank God that He *chose* YOU for such a time as this. I thank God for Beverly, who was inspired by her journey with Verity to put her life experiences into this compelling resource guide. This book will help direct and equip not only the parents but also the family, friends and caretakers who are entrusted to loving these babies as Christ loves us.

Blessings to you,

Diane P. Ferraro
CEO, Save the Storks

SECTION 1

INTRODUCTION

If you truly believe in the value of life, you care about all of the weakest and most vulnerable members of society.
–Joni Eareckson Tada, Founder and CEO, Joni & Friends

No matter how long Verity lives, she is ALREADY a blessing and a gift. She is not a mistake. Her life is not futile. As her family, we may have fears and doubts about our abilities to care for whatever her unique needs are going to be, but we don't doubt that God has beauty and purpose in all things and that He will be glorified.
–Beverly Jacobson

Chapter 1
When the Unexpected Happens

My soul melts away for sorrow;
strengthen me according to your word!
–Psalm 119:28

It was a beautiful autumn day in Glenwood, Iowa, when I received the phone call that turned my world upside down. The words *Edwards Syndrome* and *Trisomy 18* hung over me in dark clouds, obscuring my ability to think clearly. What exactly did all of this mean? The polite yet clinical voice on the other end of the phone spoke of genetic anomalies, severe difficulties and delays, likely meaning the baby I felt squirming inside my belly would not make it to birth. If she did, her life would almost certainly be brief, according to this doctor.

As my phone conversation ended that day, I was overcome by emotion yet numb at the same time. I had no idea we were embarking on a journey for which none of us had willingly purchased tickets. I could not have possibly known what lay ahead: the mental and emotional anguish; the uncertainty, fear, and anger; or—astonishingly—the unexpected, amazing love and joy, the beautiful surprises that met us along the way. All I could see in that moment was a giant, tangled mess. All I could feel was an overwhelming sense of dread.

How exactly do you move forward after your baby receives an unexpected diagnosis? How do you deal honestly with the devastation, the absolute chaos? And how in the world do you prepare to care for this child—this tiny, precious baby—when you have far more questions than answers?

More importantly, WHY move forward at all?

Why, indeed? Many in the medical community have an "easy" answer to the dilemma of a prenatal diagnosis: abortion.

Hannah went to her clinic for a routine ultrasound at 20 weeks. The appointment ended up lasting for hours, after which she was finally told, "Everything is wrong with this baby. You can't keep her." Hannah had not even learned of her daughter's Trisomy 18 diagnosis when her doctor scheduled an abortion for her. When she refused, she learned the office would not provide her with prenatal care for a child they considered "incompatible with life." Thankfully Hannah and her husband found a supportive practice, and baby Evelyn Grace was born safely at 38 weeks. Despite having only half of a heart (along with some other physical difficulties), Evelyn grew and thrived, thanks to a life-saving surgery provided early on by a cardiologist who took a chance on a baby many in the medical community had already labeled as a hopeless case.

Why did Hannah move forward with a pregnancy that involved so much risk? In her own words:

There is a great tragedy at hand when it was a thousand times easier to organize an abortion for my child than it was to find proper care to honor my pregnancy....Psalm 139 says "For you formed my inward parts; you knitted me together in my mother's womb. I praise you, for I am fearfully and wonderfully made. Wonderful are your works; my soul knows it very well." Every child. Every baby. The moment we stop defending the weakest and most vulnerable in our society will be a complete tragedy. I will always share my story. I will always stand in the gap. I will always choose life.

The fact that this book has made its way into your hands is not a coincidence. You have been given a tremendous gift—no, I'm not talking about this book, although it's my hope and prayer it will be a blessing and encouragement to you! No, the biggest gift is the precious life you are expecting. That little person may not look exactly the way you expected your son or daughter to look, and yet, here you are—already caring for your sweet baby growing inside Mama's belly.

Or perhaps your baby has already been born, and you've had the wind knocked out of you as you learned this precious little one has a life-threatening condition. Maybe you've even been told your baby's diagnosis is "incompatible with life." If that's the case, please read on, for much in this book is certainly applicable to your situation as well.

The reality is your baby is a GIFT. Let's firmly establish the truth on which you can stand when circumstances threaten to overwhelm you. This, precious one, is where my heart finally landed when I cried out to God asking Him to make sense of the situation for myself, my husband, and also for our other children. (Let's face it—this is a difficult thing for adults to understand, let alone teens and younger kids.)

If you are a Bible-believing Christian as I am, the following concepts are likely familiar to you. If you have different beliefs than mine, no worries. I hope reading over my perspective on the value of life will be helpful and perhaps give you some things to ponder as you make decisions in the days to come.

6 FOUNDATIONAL TRUTHS:

1. ***Your baby is loved.*** God's love for all humans is found throughout His entire love letter to us—the Bible. The reason we even know and experience love is because He first loved us.[1] God loves your baby even more than you do! He is just as concerned about what happens to your baby as He is about what happens in your life. (Be comforted, Mama! Be comforted, Daddy! YOU also are loved so very much!)

2. ***Your baby is special.*** In the Gospel of Matthew, Jesus is speaking to His disciples, assuring them of their worth in God's eyes. He says, "Are not two sparrows sold for a penny? And not one of them will fall to the ground apart from your Father. But even the hairs of your head are all numbered. Fear not, therefore; you are of more value than many sparrows."[2] God knows how many hairs are on your baby's head. He knows the condition of every organ, every tissue, every cell. There is no one else on earth like your baby, nor will there ever be. Your baby is special in God's eyes, far more valuable than a price tag could ever hope to convey!

3. ***Your baby is created in God's image***. We know from Genesis that God created Adam and Eve in His image. Every human being since is formed in that image. It's true that imperfections exist because we live in a sinful, fallen world that experiences the effects of people choosing to go against God's perfect plan. But whether your baby has an extra chromosome or is missing a significant body part, you can know without a doubt that your child is also an image-bearer of a loving Creator, therefore having infinite worth and value.

4. ***Your baby is fearfully and wonderfully made.*** I love Psalm 139, written by King David. In the poem, David acknowledges that God knows every single detail of his life. He contemplates the fact that God knitted him together in his mother's womb, saying, "I praise you, for I am fearfully and

wonderfully made....Your eyes saw my unformed substance; in your book were written, every one of them, the days that were formed for me, when as yet there was none of them."[3] This is true of every baby that has ever been or ever will be born!

5. ***Your baby has a purpose.*** In Psalm 57, another poem written by King David, he writes, "I cry out to God Most High, to God who fulfills His purpose for me." Speaking of David, the apostle Paul refers to him in a sermon recorded in Acts 13, saying in verse 36, "For David, after he had served the purpose of God in his own generation, fell asleep and was laid with his fathers..." Like King David, your baby will serve God's very special purpose in the world! This is true no matter how long or short your child's life is here on earth. We cannot possibly know the ripple effects our little ones will have, not only on their immediate families, but also on people we may not even meet in person. Many parents of these special babies report being changed for the better, just for having a special-needs child in their lives. Even the lives of little ones who are stillborn or pass soon after birth have deep, meaningful purpose. Parents who have chosen to carry their babies to term experience significant psychological benefits, in large part (I believe) due to the choice to allow their babies to live out their own special purposes.

6. ***Your baby will live forever.*** Regarding those who belong to Jesus, He tells His disciples, "I give them eternal life, and they will never perish, and no one will snatch them out of my hand."[4] Elsewhere in the Bible we learn that all humans have a soul which will live forever. King David grieved the loss of an infant son, telling his servants, "But now he [the child] is dead. Why should I fast? Can I bring him back again? I shall go to him, but he will not return to me."[5] We don't know how long we will have with our children here on earth—this is true whether or not they have any kind of a diagnosis! Yet we can have hope and

assurance that they will be healed and made whole, along with all who trust in Jesus, living forever in heaven.

Mama, Daddy—your baby is NOT a mistake. The anomaly, the defect, the diagnosis, whatever it is that has brought a weight to your shoulders, is not your fault. Your baby is special, so incredibly precious in the sight of a loving Creator God who never makes a mistake and never does anything without divine purpose.

Let's revisit those questions from earlier in the chapter: *How exactly does one move forward after your baby is given an unexpected diagnosis? How do you deal honestly with the devastation, the absolute chaos? And how in the world do you prepare to care for this child—this tiny, precious baby—when you have far more questions than answers?*

As we move forward in this book (and as **you** move forward into the chapters of your own unique story), let's remember the importance of that forward movement, because in the process of moving from diagnosis to delivery and beyond, you will find answers to those questions and more. I know, precious mama, how difficult it is to pick up the shattered pieces of your heart and attempt to carry on with details of life that now seem so insignificant compared to the weight pressing down on you. But you must.

It is vital for your own mental and emotional health.

It is vital for the process of preparing for what lies ahead.

And it is vital for developing the confidence you need to advocate for yourself and for your child.

Take some deep breaths. Close your eyes and just BE. Lift up your concerns in prayer. One breath at a time, one moment at a time, one day at a time. You can do this! Your baby is depending on you!

Chapter 2

Where Do We Go From Here?

Don't let anyone steal your hope. We were given nine days if that. We were blessed with nine and a half years. Our children are not defined by their diagnosis. Let your faith be bigger than your fears.
–Rachel

If you received a prenatal diagnosis, perhaps, like me, between the moment you first heard the news and the time for delivery, you'll find yourself riding a roller coaster of emotions. For me, those months seemed to stretch into eternity. Never before had I experienced such paradox. I both dreaded and anticipated the birth experience. I was weepy and emotional one day, angry and determined the next. I tossed and turned at night, unable to turn off my brain, then dozed off in the middle of a daytime activity when exhaustion overcame me. Fear seemed ever present, and yet somehow, strangely, so was peace.

I'm so glad you're here—this book is a compilation of some of the things we learned during our own roller coaster ride, concepts that would have been so helpful during those months of waiting anxiously…for what, we didn't exactly know. The not knowing was probably the most difficult aspect of the whole journey! Unfortunately, I can't give you any guarantees or clarity regarding the specifics of your own situation. However, I believe that if we examine three important phases of this journey, we can work together toward some positive outcomes no matter what the future holds. These are applicable regardless of whether your diagnosis came before or after baby's birth. Note that these broad phases we will discuss in the next major sections of this book are not necessarily linear and may overlap.

Acceptance

The first phase is ***acceptance***. As you likely already know, an important part of this journey will be coming to terms with your new reality, your new "normal." You don't have to like it! Trust me, I was kicking and screaming on this part of our path, and I confess I reverted to resistance more than a few times along the way, even after I felt I had finally made my peace with my daughter's diagnosis. And truthfully, this will be an ongoing process as you learn more and more about your baby and what exactly his or her condition will require.

For us, this may have been the most difficult part of the journey. It took some time for the truth to really sink in. Though it would have been preferable to live in denial, we knew our reality had changed, like it or not. Because of our spiritual beliefs, aborting our baby—no matter what her condition—was never an option.

And so our first step on this journey was to accept the truth about our situation. This went far beyond the diagnosis itself and into the emotional shock and grief, the ramifications, the ripple effects that were going to turn our lives upside down. I grieved the loss of my expectations for our baby. I cried at the thought of burying my little girl—and yet I also cried at the thought of caring for a child with special needs. I felt fearful for what bringing this child into the world would do to my marriage and to our other children. Everything felt so overwhelming. But I had to acknowledge and accept the truth about my fears and feelings in order to move forward in my journey.

Somewhere along the line, as we began to move past the shock of the initial diagnosis and the grief that came in various forms, I learned it is possible to ACCEPT reality while at the same time despising it with my whole being. I'll be honest: my acceptance in the beginning was not gracious. This was not a pretty phase for me. I was numb, exhausted, sad, weepy, devastated, anxious, fearful—I never knew there were so many related emotions that could overwhelm my body, mind, and soul. And yet, little by little, I inched my way toward accepting this new reality. I grew in my relationship with God as I learned to yield to HIS plans and thus truly be able to say, "Your will, not mine, be done." I accepted the fact that nothing about this pregnancy, delivery, and beyond would be what I had expected it to be. And it sounds crazy, but there was a peace in getting to that point.

Allowing yourself to settle into a place of acceptance—however reluctant it may be—is the healthy first step in your journey. On the other end of the spectrum is a dark, forbidding place of mental and emotional anguish. Because I've been there too, I urge you with all of my being to do what it takes to avoid that pit! It's okay to swing on the emotional pendulum, but don't get stuck on the far end of the arc. Remember emotions are like waves, and waves don't last forever. They roll in and out, and you can either ride them and let them take you to beautiful places or else you can be swallowed up by them, leading to even more pain and misery. In the coming chapters, we will journey toward acceptance, whatever that may look like for you.

Awareness

The second phase we will work toward is ***awareness***. I don't know how it was for you, but when we got our daughter's diagnosis, it felt as if we were standing underneath a dump truck, with mountains of statistics, handouts, scientific terms, and counseling brochures pouring down on us. As I tried to sort through it all and make some kind of sense of the dire medical jargon, I soon realized I was drowning in a sea of statistics with absolutely NO IDEA of what our own personal reality would be. I quickly became aware of my lack of knowledge, and that awareness drove me to find the community and resources we didn't even know we needed.

There were tiers of awareness, too, I discovered. Maybe it sounds strange, but just sit with this for a moment: you probably don't know how much you don't know. (The truth is, doctors don't even know how much they don't know!) Allowing yourself time to grow in your own awareness will help you avoid making decisions in haste, leading to what may very well be a lifetime of regret. I've known mamas who followed through with the only choice they felt they had—possibly the only choice their doctors gave them. They aborted a baby they were told would not survive anyway, only to learn afterward that many children with that same condition are not only *surviving*, but also *thriving* and bringing joy to their families. My heart goes out to these women. It's because I've seen their pain and anguish that I urge you to take all the time you need in order to grow in your awareness and understanding of what exactly your child's condition is. We will get to the nitty-gritty specifics later, but for now, rest in the knowledge that it's okay to not have all the answers. Give yourself time to receive what you and your baby need. Please—don't make a hasty decision based on what could very well be outdated information or biased opinion.

And may I also urge you to not make any decisions from a place of raw emotion? Sometimes we feel we must act quickly. Doctors often pressure mothers to abort their babies before they even really understand what is happening. Again, give yourself time to absorb new information, to process your emotions, and to move into a place of total awareness of what your situation is and the ramifications of all possible developments. Our goal, as you sort through all of these details, is to help you get to a new level of awareness, one that takes into account actual stories rather than only statistics, an awareness that involves real lives rather than only raw data.

Advocacy

Finally, the third phase on this journey is ***advocacy***. Once you've accepted your new reality, once you've become aware of what your and your baby's needs are, it's time to prepare and equip yourself to advocate for your child. (And be prepared—you may need to advocate for yourself as well!)

As our due date approached, I became fervently passionate about being as prepared as possible for our daughter's entrance into the world. I found research in medical journals that was as up-to-date as possible and shared the articles with my husband and our medical team. I looked at sample birth plans and crafted our own in order to be specific about our expectations and preferences. We met with a new doctor who was supportive of our decision to deliver Verity and give her every chance at a healthy, thriving life. Once Verity was born, we maintained ongoing communication with every staff member who helped care for her, and our time in the NICU was just about as positive of an experience as it could possibly be. Our new role as Trisomy advocates became entwined into our everyday life as we welcomed Verity home and settled into another "new normal," one which now involves various appointments to the specialty clinics, therapies, adaptive equipment, and so on.

You are—and always will be—your child's best advocate! It's best to walk into this with your eyes wide open. Not everyone in the world will be enthusiastic or supportive of your decision to give your baby his or her best possible life on planet earth. I had no idea the level of discrimination against babies with prenatal diagnoses, and it took me by surprise when I found myself listening to a neonatologist telling me my "retarded" daughter would live a "futile life." (True story.)

Acceptance, awareness, advocacy: these are the phases we will explore together as we work our way through this book. I'm so honored to be on this journey with you!

Chapter 3

What Are We Looking For?

Diagnosis is not prognosis.
These kids will write their own stories.
–Megan

To help you as we explore the phases we discussed in the last chapter (acceptance, awareness, and advocacy), we will dig into three important outcomes of this journey. First, we want to *center ourselves* so we can think and act in ***alignment*** with our values and worldview. Second, we desire to *educate ourselves* so we can have ***assurance*** that we are making the best decisions for our baby and our family. And third, we need to *prepare ourselves* so we can find ***significance*** in this difficult journey, knowing there is meaning and purpose no matter what happens.

Alignment

First, as you work through accepting your new reality, you may face moments of near panic, wondering if you can do this, wondering how you will get through the next weeks and months. You may be tempted to act or react in ways that are not fully aligned with your value system. Centering yourself on a firm foundation is the most important thing you can do to make certain you are thinking and acting in accordance with your beliefs and values. This is the time to examine your personal worldview and make sure it is strong enough to withstand the storms of difficulty. You see, we filter everything that happens to us and every decision we must make through the lens of our worldview. We are talking about the mindset with which you approach not only the diagnosis itself, but also your own role in this unplanned journey.

Mary, a young mother, found herself in shock when she received a life-limiting diagnosis for her baby girl about halfway through her pregnancy. As a practicing Christian who very much considered herself to be pro-life, Mary listened in stunned surprise when her medical team presented her with a seemingly easier alternative than carrying her baby to term. She remembers, "In the midst of us being in shock and cramming to figure out what to do, we had specialists giving us the option to 'induce early' at a convenient time when family could all be there, at any time, next week if wanted. At 21 weeks in my womb they offered to induce. My mind considered it for a few minutes....I have a whole new compassion for so many who are found in that same spot and do abort the given pregnancy."

Mary is not alone in feeling overwhelmed and underprepared for these circumstances. As I've already mentioned, my pregnancy was, for me, by far one of the most difficult parts of our story. Yet as I look back, it is now such an integral part of who I am, the sacred testimony of God's faithfulness leading ultimately to my spiritual and personal growth. This is true for my husband as well. We had to go on a journey not only as individuals, but also as a married couple. For us, centering ourselves on the foundational truths of the Word of

God was of the utmost importance. Truths that we previously never questioned (because they weren't challenged) suddenly lay naked before us, begging for examination.

The next section of this book will help you think through this idea of centering yourself so that you can move forward with confidence, acting in alignment with your values and beliefs. We will take a look at foundational truths on which thoughts and decisions are based. We will dig into preconceived ideas you may have when it comes to delivering and caring for a child with special needs. This may challenge you and your core beliefs—but it is difficult mental work that you must be willing to do in order to move forward in your journey with grace and ease. As we deal with personal mindset—which includes your mental, emotional, and spiritual health—we of course must also address the hard truth of living with uncertainty, which is an unavoidable part of this whole deal. Whether it's the ambiguity of whether your baby will make it alive to birth or the doubts and fears concerning what comes after delivery, uncertainty plays a major role at least for a season. We will discuss ways to make this more bearable. Defining (or redefining) your worldview and having a solid foundation at your own center is key for all of this.

Assurance

For the next step, as you educate yourself about your baby's condition and grow in awareness, the goal is that you will ultimately come to a place of peace and assurance. This is an outcome entirely independent of what happens with your baby: it is a state of mind springing from the truth of your foundation.

Undoubtedly you already realize the pressing need for specific information as you move forward—not only raw data and statistics, but also real-life stories to give you insight into what may lie ahead. In section 3, we will look at different avenues to help you on this portion of the journey. You will feel equipped for collecting the important information so necessary for you, your child, and your family. What does current medical research say about your child's diagnosis? What does your doctor say? And more than that, what do real-life parents say? This will give you a broader picture than simply the raw data given at the time of diagnosis.

The old saying "Knowledge is power" is true. Beyond that, though, we pray the knowledge you accumulate in the coming months will combine with a firm foundation of truth to bring you peace and assurance that no matter what lies ahead, you are acting in good faith on behalf of your precious little one.

Significance

And last, but certainly not least, as you prepare yourself to step into the advocate's role, our goal is that you will find deep meaning and significance in this journey itself along with whatever the outcome is. There is eternal purpose in every single life, your own as well as your baby's. As you read quotes from other parents related to specifics of this journey and consider some of their suggestions, I believe you will find your own heart opening to new hope and possibilities.

As we dig into some nitty-gritty details in the fourth section of the book, you will find yourself thinking of your own ideas to mark the significance of this journey. We will talk about how you can slow down and enjoy your pregnancy, perhaps even planning for a baby shower or celebration of the life you are carrying. We will also take a hard but necessary look at the logistics of loss and how you might plan for the unthinkable. On the other hand, I hope you will be encouraged as we discuss the many resources available to help you if you are able to bring your baby home from the hospital.

After gleaning as many facts as you can, plus learning from the stories of other parents farther along in the journey, it will be time to bring it all together to formulate a plan. While the best-laid plans can certainly go awry, in this case, leaving things to chance is definitely not an option, especially if you desire to find and experience deep meaning in this journey. From birth plans to family discussions, we will tackle the behind-the-scenes work that will help you feel confident and courageous as you become your baby's best advocate. You are speaking up for one who cannot speak for him or herself, and that role alone carries great significance. You are and will always be this child's mother or father, whether on earth or in heaven. Let that priceless gift rest on you like a crown of glory.

SECTION 2

CENTER YOURSELF

Acceptance

Accepting the inevitable early on has helped me emotionally be prepared. Going through and identifying the stages of grief has helped as much as it's able to. But most of all acceptance, that no matter what I do for her, it won't heal her or make things better for her. I tried to find a silver lining to every negative and learned to embrace each day as it came, appreciating each day she was alive up until she took her last breath on my chest.

–Flower

Chapter 4

Finding a Firm Foundation

A mother will never regret choosing life for her child, even in the most difficult circumstances. But choosing to terminate, especially if pressured by your doctor, will lead to regrets, pain, and a life filled with what ifs. Choose life!
–Candace

In chapter one we looked at six foundational truths about your baby (and all humans, in fact). Here's a quick review:

1. *Your baby is loved.*
2. *Your baby is special.*
3. *Your baby is created in God's image.*
4. *Your baby is fearfully and wonderfully made.*
5. *Your baby has a purpose.*
6. *Your baby will live forever.*

If you are a Christian who calls Jesus Christ your Lord and Savior, you are likely already very familiar with these truths. But a reminder never hurts, especially when your world has been shaken by an unexpected diagnosis.

If your belief system is not based on the Bible, then I encourage you to take time to consider what it is that serves as your foundation. Do you believe you were created by God? Or do you believe everything you see and feel and experience is the result of absolute random chance? Do you believe we are eternal beings, or does everything end at the moment of death?

The answers to those questions will necessarily lead to very different thoughts about the value of life—both here on earth and after death. If you are not convinced your baby was created by a loving God who has purpose for every human being He creates, and if you don't believe heaven and hell exist, then why not choose abortion? What value is there in this journey of carrying a fragile baby?

If, however, that fragile baby has value simply because he or she has an eternal soul, then we honor the life that exists, no matter how long or short its duration. We do what is in our power to support this little person's life and trust God—the Author of life—with the details.

A crisis such as a devastating prenatal diagnosis will often force us to examine our core beliefs in a way like never before. A person who feels strongly about the right to life may find herself shaken when faced with the fact that her own child has life-limiting anomalies or defects. On the other hand, a woman who passionately defends the choice to terminate a pregnancy for any and all reasons may find herself in a living paradox as she battles conflicting emotions—if the baby within her isn't really a baby until or unless she chooses to give birth, then why the agonizing emotional pain related to the diagnosis? Could it be that her very being—with an innate recognition of what is happening inside her own body, mind, and spirit—testifies to the value of that little life?

Feeling a live, wiggly baby while not knowing just how long he or she might be alive is such a strange, strange place emotionally and mentally. There is life—and death—all in one thought. It's enough to drive anyone to the brink. This is why it is so important that you center yourself on a foundation of truth, something strong enough to keep you standing firm when life seems to be crumbling around you.

In our culture where people are encouraged to create and speak their own truth, these words may seem strange. But I don't believe truth is relative. When I've been shaken to my core because of loss, fear, depression, anxiety, isolation, and other difficult circumstances and conditions, I have been able to press on and come through the fire only because of the foundation of truth on which I have built my life.

While I can lay out the pillars on which *my* faith rests, ultimately ***you*** have to determine what ***you*** believe. What is it that will help YOU on this journey?

In what or whom do you trust?

What determines your value—and likewise, what gives your baby value?

How do you determine your purpose for being here? Your baby's purpose?

How do you account for the suffering and difficulties of life?

Is there hope for the future, beyond this life?

I will share my answers to these questions in Appendix A if you'd like to read them and possibly study further. For now, I encourage you to spend some time pondering (and maybe praying over) how *you* would answer. Perhaps you may choose to write out a statement of faith that addresses these questions and encompasses your worldview. This would be a good exercise to do with your spouse as well. It is not uncommon for one partner to desire an abortion upon learning of a baby's genetic anomalies while the other wants to give the baby a chance. If you and your spouse—and possibly extended family members—are not on the same page with your core values and beliefs, it is crucial that you talk through these important issues sooner rather than later. Things may get more difficult and complicated as time goes on.

Sarah's testimony

Sarah, mother of Hannah Paige, shared the following in our From Diagnosis to Delivery support group some months after her sweet Hannah passed away after 13 days:

I think my greatest preparation came through some difficult times I went through a few years earlier, grappling with how God can allow such bad things to happen in this world. It's too much to relay here, but after some dark times and some wrestling (for a couple of years), I was able to come to an understanding of all I could know about the subject and see how extremely bad things could actually be worth it for all people involved. The result was my faith became stronger, and I could see the value of suffering. Part of this came through revisiting why we can trust that the Bible is God's Word and studying what the Bible says about eternal rewards.

When we received this difficult diagnosis, I completely fell back on that knowledge and came to accept what was happening. I knew God wasn't allowing this to happen because of anything I did or did not do, and that I was not exempt from experiencing deep suffering (though we all go through different types). Knowing TRUTH from God's Word helped me keep my mind in the right place, for the most part. I did have my moments though, thinking, "I don't want a baby with Down syndrome!" and "This is not what I signed up for!" Theology and truth was truly my greatest comfort. I would lie in bed and just "be," knowing God was with me in my trial even when I couldn't pray. I tried to enjoy every little kick and movement, and I treasure those memories.

Centered on a foundation of truth

As I've gotten older, I find some morning yoga helps to keep my body from feeling achy and creaky. I've learned I need to be intentional to strengthen and work my core especially or else I am prone to back pain. During one workout, the instructor talked about "centering" ourselves, a phrase I tended to roll my eyes at in the past. But as the session went on, she encouraged us to move from our center—to focus on our core and initiate movement from there. I followed her instructions. And you know what? I could feel the difference. My back was no longer bearing the brunt of the work. Moving from my center, my core, not only changed the way I moved through the remainder of the workout, it also spilled over into my everyday activities. It affected my posture, the way I lifted objects, even the way I got up from a chair. When I am intentional to "move from my center," I have a strength from my core foundation that allows me to move through my day with grace and ease.

As you navigate this journey with your special baby, may I encourage you to "move from your center?" Strengthen your core foundation. Be intentional. Make thoughtful decisions from a place of calm and clarity rather than from the fog of emotions. If your center is feeling shaky, it's probably time to begin a "daily workout routine." Exercise your faith, perhaps beginning with a heart-to-heart conversation with God, who already knows your heart and desires to have a relationship with you.

Let us fix our eyes on Jesus, the author and perfecter of our faith, who for the joy set before him endured the cross, scorning its shame, and sat down at the right hand of the throne of God. Consider him who endured such opposition from sinful men, so that you will not grow weary and lose heart.
–Hebrews 12:2-3, NIV

Chapter 5
Dealing with Emotions

It's ok not to be ok. I always thought I had to be ok, but the diagnosis is a lot to digest. Be open and talk about it. It will not only help you to stop crying, it will educate so many people.
–Jayda

Twice I experienced early miscarriages. Those losses affected me profoundly, and I definitely grieved the loss of those little ones. And yet I was completely unprepared for the level of anguish my husband and I experienced while still carrying a living child. I felt a depth of loss and sadness I had never encountered before. I have since learned I was not alone in those feelings by any means.

Receiving a life-limiting diagnosis for your baby throws everything—*everything*—into a new light. You are torn between shopping for the nursery and planning a memorial service. You don't know whether to have a baby shower or look for a burial gown. Life plans come to a halt, for there is simply no way to know what you will or won't be able to do in the future.

For those who have no other children at this time, there is a sense of loss of a "normal" baby experience—a normal pregnancy, baby shower, labor and delivery experience, coming home celebration, and so on. For all parents, the loss extends to the hopes and dreams they had for their child from the moment they saw those lines on the pregnancy test. Unending questions consume all waking thoughts.

Will my child make it to birth?
How long will we have with our baby?
What will my child actually be capable of doing?
How severe ARE these physical anomalies, anyway?
What will life look like if we bring our baby home?
What about my other children?
What about future children?
Can we afford what our child will need?
What medical decisions might we have to make?

Trying to deal with even ONE of those questions (or a thousand others that aren't even listed) is overwhelming. When you feel bombarded by these questions and thoughts every waking moment—well, *overwhelming* doesn't begin to describe it. Besides the list of unknowns, emotions blindside you out of nowhere, often in a seemingly paradoxical way. Your body may very well react to the onslaught, too. This level of trauma affects us physically, mentally, emotionally, and spiritually.

Does the word *trauma* seem extreme? If you're in the throes of processing a diagnosis, you likely agree with me that it isn't. Let us first acknowledge the fact that your situation is, in fact, traumatic. A dictionary definition of the word tells us you are undergoing "an experience that produces psychological injury or pain." Rather than attempting to downplay our feelings, let's honor them as an authentic response to an extremely difficult and emotionally intense situation. Suppressing feelings leads to further complications, including physical problems that may not show immediately.

Before we examine some of the feelings that seem to be common with a prenatal diagnosis, please consider two observations about feelings and emotions:

1. They are not, in and of themselves, right or wrong. They just ARE. How we choose to react in response to those feelings, though, is where we need to be careful, because actions have consequences. Don't be afraid or ashamed of any of your feelings, but do be careful of what might follow those feelings. This leads to the next observation…

2. Feelings and emotions are often extremely strong right at first. When you feel overwhelmed, remember that you are likely at the peak of whatever it is you are feeling—the intensity WILL taper off. I'm not saying it will go away, but at some point the high emotions will level off or possibly even morph into something altogether different.

In light of the above, it is extremely important to refrain from taking any significant actions in the midst of heightened sentiments. Too often we regret those choices later on, when we are thinking more clearly and have more control over our thoughts and feelings.

Now let's move on for a brief look at some common feelings that come when we receive a life-limiting diagnosis for our baby. These are listed in no particular order—you may find yourself dealing with one or more at any given time.

Denial

This can't be happening. We still have a 1 in 10 chance that our baby is all right. It was four excruciatingly long days between the time I heard about my blood test raising suspicions about Trisomy 18 and our diagnostic ultrasound. Denial was in full force. But the ultrasound findings showed some abnormalities. We chose to do an amniocentesis. Yet even when the diagnosis was confirmed, it was easier to retreat mentally into denial than deal with this scary news head on. While the tendency to deny reality is a perfectly human reaction, a self-protective instinct, it's not likely to last long in this situation. Pregnancy seems to last forever, but we all know there is a limited time for our baby to remain in the safety of the womb. At some point, ready or not, we find ourselves moving on to our next step.

Guilt

As moms, we know this feeling all too well. When a prenatal diagnosis is present, sometimes the tendency is to wonder what we did wrong. Perhaps physically, we think about various choices we've made, questioning whether something we did caused harm to our baby. Was it something I ate? Drank? Too much physical activity? Not enough? Let me gently reassure you—you are not to blame for gene variations or mutations! In some cases it is possible a parent is a carrier for a particular condition (though not affected himself/herself). However, even in these situations, you are not to blame! You can't change your own genetic code!

Guilt can also come in this form: *What did I do wrong?* As in, *what am I being punished for*? In this twisted emotional state, we assume a bad situation is the result of a cause we could have controlled. Let me say it again: you are NOT to blame! You are NOT being punished. Your baby is a gift, no matter what his or her condition. If you are blaming yourself for some reason, go back to those foundational truths we discussed in the last chapter. Set your mind on positive truisms, perhaps creating affirmation statements to read and meditate on throughout the day. (My personal affirmations come from Scripture verses. I found the book of Psalms spoke to my soul during the difficult days of my pregnancy with Verity.)

Anger

Anger may surface at any point in this journey and is often related to one or more other emotions. It might be directed at a spouse, another family member, a doctor, or even a well-meaning friend who says the "wrong" thing. It's also not uncommon to feel angry with God. *"Why did you let this happen to me?"* Perhaps there is resentment toward those with "normal" pregnancies or babies, or feelings of bitterness toward those who don't seem to care or understand what you're going through. While these are normal, understandable feelings, it's important not to stay in that volatile state. Recognize it for what it is and see if you can dig through the anger and identify the emotion behind it. Did you snap at your spouse because deep down you're fearful for what will happen to your marriage? Are you ready to bite your friend's head off because you're fighting off a growing sense of guilt?

Remember our admonition earlier—not to act in the height of emotions? This is especially important when the emotion is anger! If you find yourself struggling with unexpected bouts of anger, first acknowledge the feeling and see if you can find the root cause. Then find a healthy, safe way to deal with it. Can you go for a walk? Take a hot bath? Close your eyes and breathe deeply? Pray or journal? The moment will pass. If it's more than a moment—if you begin to feel out of control (whether because of anger or any other emotion)—don't be afraid to reach out for help. A trusted pastor or mentor or even a professional counselor or therapist would be glad to walk this journey with you.

Isolation

"The feeling of isolation at the time of diagnosis is almost universal among parents," says Patricia McGill Smith, author of the helpful article "You Are Not Alone."[1] I wish I could say this feeling only comes along with receiving your baby's diagnosis, but the fact is, no matter what lies before you, this journey is fraught with loneliness. If your baby makes it to birth and beyond, you will feel isolated because you are raising a child with special needs. If your baby is stillborn or passes away after birth, you will feel isolated because you will bear a grief that not everyone around you understands. I don't say this to overwhelm or burden you, by any means. But if you can tuck this nugget away, it will not come as such a shock to your system when you are feeling alone and stranded in the desert of difficulty.

Knowing this is part of this journey can help you bolster your support system sooner rather than later. Make sure you are working on your relationship with your spouse. Communicate, communicate, communicate! Share with a trusted friend or two your deepest emotions related to this journey. And most importantly, find your tribe, those parents whose children have the same or a similar diagnosis as yours. Some of those folks you will likely never meet in person, but those online relationships can be a lifeline to you and your family. No matter what the diagnosis, there is someone else out there who can relate to your struggles—likely many someones! There is no greater relief than those "me too" moments when you hear others saying the very words you yourself would say.

Fear

As humans, we fear the unknown far more than what we do know. And so much is unknown when it comes to carrying a baby with a complex medical diagnosis. Our fears are fueled by horror stories we find online, negative predictions by medical personnel, or even unsupportive friends or family.

At the beginning of our journey, in those first days and weeks following the diagnosis, I mostly feared having to bury my baby. We didn't expect her to live to birth or much beyond based on the information we were finding at the time. But after a couple of months, after we had stumbled upon some online support groups, I faced a deeper fear, an ugly fear I didn't even want to put into words. I saw photos and videos of children with the same diagnosis as our daughter, and they were living and thriving. And while my heart began to sing with hope, wondering if our story might take a similar turn, deep down I began to question whether I was capable of caring for a special-needs child. I was already overwhelmed with the 8 children in my house—how in the world would I manage with one who clearly would have some significant needs and developmental delays? I finally had to admit my deepest fear was not that my child would die—but that she would live. I felt ashamed of my selfishness. Yet when I confessed my horrid thoughts in blog form, I found that I was certainly not alone in this fear. Naming and admitting it brought relief. It didn't solve anything in that moment, but I was able to move forward, choosing to believe that God would provide me with whatever I needed to take care of our daughter.

Knowing fear is normal doesn't make it easier to cope with. But we don't have to allow fear to control our lives. I have found bringing my fears into the open, sharing them with trusted loved ones and mentors, diffuses the ugly, life-sucking thoughts that grip my soul. You don't have to have all the answers lined up in order to be free from fear. Breathe deeply. Find joy and gratitude right where you are. And consciously release those fears to a loving God who tells us 365 times in the Bible to "fear not."

Grief

Brooke shares, "Phoenix is my first child. I'm still navigating how to be a new parent and a special-needs parent at the same time. And, I'll be very frank, I grieve not having a normal experience with childbirth. I grieve not being in the hospital for three or four days and having the happy sendoff—put your baby in the car seat and they send you off. It wasn't like that for us. I grieve not having that experience."

Receiving a life-limiting diagnosis for your baby brings grief on various levels. You may find yourself grieving a loss that hasn't even happened yet. Certainly there is the loss of expectations for your child and the life you imagined for him or her. And as Brooke shared, you may grieve having to exchange the experience you wanted for what fell into your lap instead. Unfortunately, this is not an emotion that will quietly go to the far corners of the closet and be quiet. No matter what you encounter in the future, grief will always be lurking. If your child is born alive and comes home from the hospital, grief will hit you an unexpected moments when you remember this is a "life-limiting diagnosis." It will blindside you when you learn of a child with the same diagnosis passing away. It will walk alongside fear as you wonder when it will happen to you.

And of course…the unthinkable may very well happen. You may choose to carry your child to term only to go through the agony of a stillbirth. Or maybe you get a few hours or a few days with your little one before that precious soul slips away to heaven. Barb, mother of Stacy, had nearly 37 years with her special-needs daughter, but she is quick to say no matter how much time we have here on earth with our loved ones, "It's never enough." Our time on earth is brief in light of eternity. Losing a child is a grief unlike any other. No one can say whether that burden will be yours to carry, or how long you might have to carry it. Yet it is not helpful to live in the *what ifs*. As Barb also says, "Many of our children write their own book."

A comforting reminder to me personally is this verse: "Therefore do not worry about tomorrow, for tomorrow will worry about itself. Each day has enough trouble of its own."[2]

Processing emotions

How do you best work through complex issues and emotions? Are you a writer? A reader? A verbal processor? Personally, I found writing to be my best outlet. Probably the best thing I did for myself mentally and emotionally was start a blog. I then journaled everything about my pregnancy, the diagnosis, and all the information coming at us, as well as my emotional responses to each topic. (This also served as a way to keep our loved ones updated on our situation without the emotional investment of repeating information.) I encourage you to find an outlet that will be helpful and even therapeutic for you as you sort through your emotions as well as track the information you receive.[3] Whether you write your deepest thoughts in a special notebook or regularly meet a trusted friend to cry over coffee, you need to be intentional about allowing yourself to THINK and to FEEL.

As an aside, my blog was not only my emotional outlet, but it also became more than I ever imagined it would be. I thought I was simply recording my own personal journey. Little did I know God would use those writings to bless and encourage others walking through similar difficulties. And now that Verity has been with our family for some years, the blog I started in the fall of 2016 is a beautiful collection of memories, a testimony to God's faithfulness and the hope we have no matter the circumstances. My raw, emotional journal entries became the seeds of a purposeful ministry. It's worth considering—how might YOUR journey affect others in a positive way? While you may not be able to see past the next hour, let alone the next year, remember that regardless of what happens, time will pass, and at some point you will be on the other side of this particular part of the journey. Your experiences and feelings now can be used to help others later.[4]

Gratitude

One final thought as we close this chapter: a powerful choice you can make is to live in gratefulness. I encourage and even challenge you to start a gratitude journal if you don't already do this. Put it on your night stand and take a few minutes every morning or evening (or both) to write at least 3-5 things for which you are grateful. This exercise will create more room for love, joy, peace, and other positive feelings. It doesn't mean the anger, fear, and grief will disappear, but it does help shape your perspective and help you find your strength and courage.

What are you grateful for today?

I think some of the greatest advice I was given in the NICU was from Nurse Mary. She told me to allow myself to grieve the things that will not be, but more importantly, celebrate all that is! It's so important to live with a grateful heart! Every day with a special needs child is a gift straight from heaven. Choose joy!

–Heidi

Chapter 6

Living with Uncertainty

Uncertainty is the only certainty there is.
Knowing how to live with insecurity is the only security.
–Mathematician John Allen Paulos

Many moms report that not knowing what will happen with their babies is the hardest part of receiving a life-limiting diagnosis. As part of the human race, it seems we all deal with "control issues" to one extent or another! We are designed to seek knowledge to help us navigate the future in safe and meaningful ways.

When our uncertainty leads us to learn more about our child's condition, form a birth plan, and prepare for whatever it is we may face in the coming months, we are moving forward in acceptance of our situation. But if we allow ourselves to be paralyzed by that uncertainty, then we will find ourselves in a cycle of uncontrollable emotions, with anxiety being the tip of the iceberg. If you find yourself feeling frustrated or worried about not having all the answers, take some time to ponder the points in this chapter. Since this is a part of the journey you simply can't avoid, let's take the edge off the pain and find ways to co-exist with uncertainty.

Uncertainty is an unavoidable part of life.

Working with moms who have been given a prenatal diagnosis (and having been one myself), I have found a perspective that is common (although not necessarily universal). Sometimes we seem to think the next ultrasound, the upcoming fetal echocardiogram, the appointment with the geneticist or neonatologist—whatever is scheduled next—will answer those pressing questions and help us know what to expect. Usually, however, we find ourselves with even more questions! As our due date approached, I felt a mounting anxiety over the birth experience, wanting to know just what it was our baby would need and how things would go. I felt if we could just get past delivery, life would get easier because we would KNOW about our sweet girl. The fact is, uncertainty continues to be a part of our lives. Granted, it does not rule the day the way it did during my pregnancy with Verity—so in one sense it does get a bit easier as you move into a new normal. Just know that it never magically disappears.

Uncertainty is a normal part of life.

When we are undergoing a personal crisis, we naturally turn inward as a self-protective measure. This causes us to feel isolated and alone, as we tend to forget other people and their own worries. Remembering that uncertainty in some form will always be present in our human experience can help us live with the tension it brings. Donnovan Somera Yisrael, senior health educator at Stanford University, says, "The challenge is to begin to accept that uncertainty and change are a normal part of life and understand how to reframe our thinking so we can live without constantly dreading the inevitable."[1] Yisrael reminds us that even though we tend to think of uncertainty and stress as negative, they only take whatever power we give them. As an example, he observes that we enjoy attending social events and watching sports and TV shows because we don't know what's going to happen. We may be nervous at potential negative outcomes, but we're also excited about the possibility of positive outcomes. What is the most positive outcome you can imagine for you and your child? Allow yourself to think about that while acknowledging possible negative outcomes, on which we tend to fixate. Reframing uncertainty in our own minds can shift us from a negative to a positive mindset.

While uncertainty is a normal part of life, what may be throwing you off guard is that prior to now, you may not have ever heard of your baby's diagnosis. Not only are you uncertain about what is coming next, but you are in utterly uncharted territory. It's one thing to be unsure of where your family will live next year because your military husband is awaiting orders and it's time once again to relocate. It's another thing entirely when you enter a world you never knew existed. Even if you had a passing awareness of the medical condition, chances are, it has not entered your own personal world in such a significant way. However, you can know with certainty that you are not alone! Other parents are reeling with shock just as you are. Find your community!

If you haven't yet found Verity's Village, our non-profit organization would love to walk with you through this journey and can introduce you to others in this unique situation. There is support available for those who choose it.[2]

We choose how we meet with uncertainty.

Resistance or acceptance? Ironically, the more we focus on the uncertainty we are facing, the more anxious and resistant we will become. The challenging emotions we discussed in the last chapter will feel heightened, showing the truth of the saying that "what we resist persists." But there's a better way. Acceptance frees us to move forward, receiving (instead of resisting) whatever is happening in the moment. This is not the same as resigning ourselves to our fate. Accepting our situation and our feelings about it does not mean it will never get better. We can't know the future, but we *can* choose how we live in the present.

Uncertainty does not equate to helplessness.

"I'm working so hard on staying in the moment and being grateful for each and every moment. It gets hard though, to be honest. Knowing I have no control and am powerless over the outcome is heart wrenching at times," says Erin, new mom to Brooklyn. Perhaps the hardest aspect of living in uncertainty is feeling we have no control over our circumstances. Experts encourage us to find the areas in which we CAN control and focus on those. In Erin's case, she is choosing to be present in the moment and practice gratitude, channeling her thoughts and energy into seemingly small things she can control while realizing she can't directly control what happens with her sweet daughter.

In the situation of a prenatal diagnosis, perhaps one of the most important areas in which you can exert control over your situation is to educate yourself as much as possible about your child's condition. But there are plenty of other, smaller ways to take control. Here are some ideas to get you started:

- Create a morning routine if you don't already have one.
- Write in a gratitude journal at least 3 things you are thankful for each day.
- Exercise—go for a walk, do some yoga, swim laps, or do another gentle activity that helps both your body and your mind.

- Be mindful about the foods you choose for fueling your body.
- Stay hydrated. (I know, I know…this is hard for a pregnant woman who is already spending a lot of time in the bathroom!)
- Avoid toxic situations and people. Be polite yet firm.
- Meditate on Scripture.
- Write out positive affirmations and incorporate them into your daily routine.
- Put boundaries on your phone time—have set times when you put your phone away and don't look at social media or answer messages. (Perhaps make a rule to not look at your phone for at least an hour after waking each morning and in the hour before going to bed.)
- Schedule time for self-care. Read a book, take a hot bath, get your hair or nails done, grab a friend and go out for lunch or coffee.

Uncertainty is exhausting.

Along with my homeschooled children, I recently learned in our science reading that brain cells need twice as much energy as other body cells because they are active all the time in everything we do. I actually paused in our reading to absorb that information. I thought, "No wonder we were so exhausted during my pregnancy with Verity!" Our brains were on overload, processing the diagnosis, what it meant for our family, what to do, how to prepare—on top of all the normal activities of daily life. We don't often think about how hard our brains work for us physically. Add emotions to the equation plus our tendency to constantly run through various scenarios, imagining possible outcomes, and it's a wonder our heads stay attached! When I share with women who are carrying a baby with a life-limiting diagnosis, I encourage them, "Give yourself lots of space and lots of grace!" This is a lot to process. If at all possible, cut out extra activities so you can get physical rest. Choose healthy ways to process your emotions as well as all the information coming at you.

Uncertainty is part of a meaningful life.

Significance and purpose drive our lives. When we feel life is chaotic and random without any meaning behind what happens or why it happens, we lose hope and feel our choices and even our lives don't really matter. The last point in this chapter takes us back to the importance of the foundational truths on which we build our lives. If your worldview doesn't allow for uncertainty and difficult times—if it can't ascribe meaning and purpose for hardships—then may I gently suggest it's a worldview that is too small. Life is complex, too much so to be a series of random mutations and chaotic events. Lean into the truth that you are loved and cared for by a sovereign God who works all things out for His glory and our good.

Chapter 7
Unpacking Preconceived Ideas

I was told at my 20 week ultrasound that my daughter had trisomy 18 and asked when I would like to abort. We chose life, and I am so glad I didn't listen to that doctor. I am sure many more parents would choose life if doctors wouldn't scare them. I am sure many more babies would be born alive if parents are given the option of intervention!

–Cat

As you travel on the road to accepting your situation—the life-limiting diagnosis of your baby and all of the ramifications packed along with it—at some point you will find yourself wrestling with your own preconceived ideas as well as those of everyone else. Let's start from the outside perspectives and work our way into our own hearts and minds.

Preconceived ideas of the medical world

Possibly the most prevalent idea that will surface after a prenatal diagnosis is that aborting your baby is the only logical option. When the medical team you trust is telling you that your child will suffer if he or she makes it to term; when an experienced doctor says your baby has no chance of survival; when everything you're reading says your baby's condition is "incompatible with life"—well, it can be a frighteningly easy path to abortion.

In one survey, 90 percent of doctors indicated abortion was justifiable in the case of what is considered "fatal" anomalies, while 63 percent felt it was justifiable for nonfatal anomalies.[1] If physicians personally feel inclined in this direction, it makes sense that their counsel to patients will be biased toward abortion as an expected and even humane choice given the circumstances. And that is in fact the experience of many women who receive a prenatal life-limiting diagnosis for their babies. What follows is a sampling of answers from women who responded to a survey in our online support groups From Diagnosis to Delivery and Rare Trisomy Parents.

*I never **felt** pressured, but they offered [abortion] first before answering any of my questions or assessing my emotional/mental state.* –Katie

We were offered termination so many times. The geneticist told us multiple times that we could "meet our baby anytime" and that our baby was incompatible with life. –Jade

We were advised every appointment up until like 26 weeks, even when we made it clear we would not terminate. When we met with the geneticist, he told us to terminate three times in our 45-minute conversation, and that was pretty much all he brought to the table, no real information. –Shea

They all tried to pressure me into it until I was 24 weeks and it was no longer legal in Georgia. –Jessica

My first OB urged me to abort Lavender. She wouldn't continue my care and even told me she would schedule my D&C. Her practice is affiliated with a religious hospital, so she was going to tell them I miscarried. It was a total out of body experience. It will forever haunt me. –Rose

Again, this is just a sampling of what many mothers have experienced. While we cannot know exact statistics here, it's not far-fetched to conclude that perhaps NOT being encouraged toward an abortion in the situation of a prenatal diagnosis might be the exception rather than the norm. Perhaps you have already had such a conversation with your medical provider. If not, do be prepared. Even if you have a supportive doctor from the beginning, it is possible you will meet with other specialists on your journey who have their own preconceived ideas about the value and potential of your baby and are not hesitant to speak their minds.

We were blessed to have a compassionate genetic counselor who met with us both before and after we received confirmation of the full trisomy 18 diagnosis for our daughter. She was incredibly kind and encouraging, noting that her role was not to direct us in what to do but simply to offer information. We were quick to tell her (as we told all medical professionals we met) that for us, abortion was not an option and that our goal was to be as informed as possible so we could prepare for whatever might happen. The counselor offered us as much positive information as she could find regarding babies with the same diagnosis, saying, "I want to give you as much of the good as I can, because I know you'll hear plenty of the bad from other places."

She wasn't wrong.

I met with the head neonatologist at the hospital where we were to deliver and was utterly unprepared for the experience. Ostensibly I was supposed to be learning what we might expect when Verity was born, what types of support she might need, how they would care for her in the NICU, and so on. However, the whole debacle instead found me listening in stunned silence as the man talked about my "retarded" daughter and the "futile life" she would live, which would require "buy-in" from the family because of the "mental, emotional, and financial drain" that it would be to have Verity in our lives.

I wish I could say I kept my composure and responded with some well-researched, pointed remarks, but the truth is I was caught so completely off guard that I couldn't even formulate words in my own brain, let alone speak them. It wasn't until I was driving home, shaking with anger and wiping away my tears, that I thought of all the things I could have or should have said.

This brings us to another aspect of preconceived ideas in the medical world, which is assuming a full understanding of another person's quality of life. Bridget Mora, community education and communications coordinator for the nonprofit ministry Be Not Afraid, observes that when medical professionals use terms such as "incompatible with life," it is often a reflection of a physician's personal judgment of the potential quality of life for that individual. Such terms do not comprise an actual medical diagnosis, yet they may become a self-fulfilling prophecy when treatments given to other babies are withheld from those with a life-limiting diagnosis.[2]

The professionals with whom you will interact on this journey all come to the table with their own education, experiences, opinions, and biases. Based on the above, they will also have their own preconceived ideas of what will or won't happen with your baby and what you should or shouldn't do. Remembering this basic fact will help you receive medical input during your appointments and then calmly take time to dissect it and compare it with your own research and "mama gut" instincts. It is quite possible you and your medical team will be on the same page from Day One. However, it is also possible that you will need to wade through a variety of opinions and resources in order to find common ground.

Preconceived ideas of family and friends

Before we chose to share the news of our baby's diagnosis with family and friends, we first had to let it sink into our own hearts and minds. When we did share, we carefully selected close family members and friends whom we could trust with the sensitive information. We waited until later—quite a bit later—before sharing with our larger community. For us, we reached a point where we decided the more people who could be praying for and supporting us, the better! However, some people choose to keep a diagnosis like this confidential for various reasons, and that is okay too. If you don't have a supportive circle, this may be the better road to take, actually, especially given the preconceived ideas you may bump up against.

Those in your closest circles will naturally share your burden to a certain extent. Out of love and concern for you, they may wish to protect you from the pain caused by learning your little one has a life-limiting diagnosis. This may take different forms.

It's not uncommon for loved ones, even spouses, to urge an abortion in this situation. Sometimes this sentiment does spring from pure intentions; however, most people have not taken the time to research and likely don't understand that actually, carrying a baby to term is not only physically safe for the mother, but also provides her with mental, emotional, and psychological benefits. Heidi Faith, founder of Still Birthday, notes, "When a mother reacts to being faced with the decision of the duration of life in utero by not completing the duration of the pregnancy to its fullest, she can face tremendous psychospiritual and/or social issues—some of which have been proven through biophysical research to be alleviated should she choose to face the duration of the pregnancy instead."[3]

Aborting a child, even one who is not expected to live long, brings a whole other set of complications and grief. Many mothers who choose abortion in these circumstances often find support groups for parents of children with the same diagnosis as the aborted baby had—and they express grief anew as they learn that maybe, just maybe, their own little one could have survived if given the opportunity.

Another preconceived idea, one which I personally encountered, is that of people in your circles hoping or praying for "complete healing." Let's be clear: I'm not opposed to anyone praying for healing for our babies, nor do I think it's impossible for healing to take place. (I've heard too many testimonies to think otherwise!) Remember our foundation of truth—I believe in a loving, all-powerful God. And sometimes God chooses to bring about a miraculous healing for His glory.

But. Not always. And…may I boldly say? Not often.

In our case, sweet Verity was diagnosed with full trisomy 18. This means that in every single cell of her body, she has an extra copy of the eighteenth chromosome. This causes a range of difficulties, a wide spectrum not unlike what we now know to be the autism spectrum. Each child is affected differently—like all of us, each child with an extra chromosome (no matter which number) is unique. So when I pondered the idea of Verity being "healed" from Edwards Syndrome, it didn't make sense to me that God would create her on purpose with an extra eighteenth chromosome and then decide to remove it!

I appreciated my friends' comments, their sympathy for our situation and desire to see good come out of it all. And yet somehow it didn't feel right. I found myself having to examine my own preconceived ideas about miracles and healing. It was one of multiple spiritual wrestling matches with God. (If you'd like to see where I landed on this particular issue, you can read more in Appendix B.)

So what to do with the preconceived ideas that form the basis for the way our loved ones interact with us? My recommendation—take them with a grain of salt. Recognize them for what they most likely are: opinions from people who truly do care for you and perhaps just aren't sure how to handle the situation. Maybe you first need to give yourself some space. Cry, journal, take some time to process what is happening. Give yourself time to let emotions settle. Then, perhaps, if the relationship warrants, gently probe into the underlying assumptions that are propping up the words you're hearing. The conversation which follows will likely indicate whether the other party truly has your best interests at heart. If not, it may be time to draw some firm boundaries for your own sanity and peace of mind.

Preconceived ideas of your own

As mentioned in Chapter 5, one of the most unsettling parts of my pregnancy with Verity was getting a look at my own thoughts, including the deepest, darkest fears lurking in my heart and mind. First I wrestled through the idea that the child I felt somersaulting in my belly would receive a burial instead of a baby shower. This, of course, was based on the preconceived ideas of those in the medical world who labeled Trisomy 18 as a condition that is "incompatible with life." After doing my own research and connecting with other families online, I became aware of a new and frightening thought. While I had wrestled and somewhat come to terms with the very real possibility that our baby might die…

…I found myself now completely terrified that she might live.

At first it was the tiniest little niggle at the back of my brain. While I felt hope when learning of other children living with the same condition as Verity, right alongside that hope was fear. I stuffed it for a long time, refusing to call it out for what it really was. And finally I had to face myself, acknowledge that as difficult as it was to admit, the truth was that I felt afraid to be the mother of a child with special needs. Once I put words to it, I was devastated to discover that ugliness inside my heart. I was ashamed of what I felt it revealed about me: weakness of character, of faith.

I'm going to share a portion of a blog post written when I was fighting with this issue. It is my hope that glimpsing my personal struggle will encourage you wherever you are today.

I know special-needs families LOVE their children. Life revolves around serving these vulnerable, precious ones, and they wouldn't trade it for anything. I see, hear, feel the love as they talk or type about their children. I already love Verity, and I wouldn't trade this for my own plans—I know that God's plans and ways are much higher than ours.

I know. I know. I KNOW.

But.

Sigh.

Someday maybe I won't need the ***but***. *Today is not that day. Today I look ahead and see real possibility of a life centered around medical appointments and special equipment for our special girl. I see lack of sleep, lack of order, lack of energy for my marriage and our other kids—our eight other precious kids. Certainly no room for a business or ministry outside my home. Sure, I also see a lot of growth and compassion and love. But. (There's that word again.) It comes with a huge dose of exhaustion and ever-present concern.*

And I am utterly, completely overwhelmed.

Oh, precious mama. Am I alone? Or have I hit on something you too have felt in your soul? I suspect my feelings are actually common…just not commonly discussed. I was afraid and ashamed to admit how fearful and overwhelmed I was at the thought of bringing Verity home from the hospital with all her special needs—and we didn't even know what they would be for certain.

Looking back, I have such compassion for where I was in that season. Of COURSE I was fearful. Of COURSE I was overwhelmed. Who wouldn't be?! There might be only a handful of people on the planet who have actually asked to be the parent of a child with special needs, and they are the saints who choose to adopt special children because God has grown in them a heart to do so. Most of us get into this gig because we were thrust into it. But you know what? We grow into it as well. We grow in our knowledge, our faith, our strength. We take it one day at a time. We learn what we need to know when we need to know it. And soon, we are living this new normal and feeling quite…*normal.*

Love blossoms.

Joy returns.

Beauty abounds.

We revel in the daily miracles others take for granted. And we smile when we think back to the preconceived ideas that brought such anxiety and fear. Now we know better, because we have been utterly undone and remade, shaped into a new purpose and passion.

Mama, I hope this encourages you. Don't be afraid to put words to your fears and concerns. You are not alone.

SECTION 3

EDUCATE YOURSELF

Awareness

The best thing you can do is educate yourself and advocate with a passion that can't be ignored. Expect to experience prejudice and cynicism about full intervention, but try to have patience and handle this with grace. The next case to follow may be met with more compassion and optimism. You know your child better than anybody. Don't let somebody make decisions on your behalf that you will regret later.

–Christina

Chapter 8

What Does Current Research Say?

I would have told my past self to enjoy my pregnancy and announce his diagnosis; research but don't obsess over trying to know everything; and lastly, go with the flow. All these babies are so different, and no one can predict your baby's future.
–Megan

It's time to get into the nitty-gritty details of this journey. You may very well still be coming to terms with your baby's diagnosis, still struggling to accept your new reality. And that's okay. But at some point, when you're ready, you have to dig in and do the hard work of becoming an expert in all things related to your special child. This is far more important than a high school research paper; however, it's worth keeping some basic principles of research in mind as you go through this process. While it is beyond the scope of this book to provide current information about multiple types of life-limiting diagnoses, we can certainly give valuable insights into the way you go about your research.

Know what you're looking for.

What questions do you have right now? A broad, vague search about your baby's condition may lead to feelings of being overwhelmed and frustrated. If you haven't already, start a journal or create a notebook or file where you can write out your questions along with the various answers you find—for you likely WILL find different answers depending on the sources!

Make sure the information is up-to-date.

What does medical literature have to say **currently** about your child's diagnosis? When we examine this question, let's remember that Dr. Google is not necessarily the expert. I made the mistake of using the internet to "research" Trisomy 18 after getting that phone call from our doctor. Since we had to wait several days before our diagnostic ultrasound, I thought I'd see what I could learn in the meantime. What I found was hardly encouraging—grim, gruesome pictures and dire phrases offering little if any hope for positive outcomes.

Perhaps you've taken a similar path. It's not wrong to utilize the power of the internet to find information. However, make sure to note the dates of any research to determine whether what you're reading is current or whether it is possibly out-of-date information. It took me awhile to realize that much of the information I found was actually based on old data, which in turn causes many to have negative preconceived ideas about the potential for babies with this diagnosis. Keep in mind the speed at which our scientific knowledge grows these days with advances in technology. An expert in the field of research tells me that the rule of thumb is ten years. If an article was written ten or more years ago, the results and recommendations may already be out of date. Seek out follow-up research that may clarify or give nuance to original conclusions.

There are many examples of parents working with medical providers who have never actually cared for a patient with their baby's condition. This means they are working from whatever information they received during their medical training—or perhaps even their own quick research once YOU entered the scope of their practice. It is possible, of course, that you have connected with a medical team already well-versed in your child's condition. If not, be prepared to learn right along with the doctors...and don't be afraid to bring in more current research! You would not be the first to gently point out the survival rates of children with [insert condition here] are actually higher than was once believed!

Find multiple sources.

Just as an academic paper cannot rely on a single resource for valid, credible points, so you cannot rely on a single study or opinion when it comes to drawing conclusions about the life of your baby. The more information you can collect, the more complete picture you will have of the range of possibilities for your child's life—and there is almost always a range. Beware when you read or hear about a definite projected outcome, whether positive or negative.

Along with this, always consider the source—for what reason are they sharing information about this diagnosis? For example, on a major abortion provider's website, the story is told of a mother who learned after a 20-week ultrasound that her daughter would be born with a complication called congenital diaphragmatic hernia (CDH). According to this article, the baby would "suffocate at birth." Supposedly, the only option was to terminate the pregnancy. This website provides no context, no specifics, no scientific data—only a heart-wrenching story of what this source obviously considers a justifiable abortion.[1]

No doubt—any life-limiting diagnosis for a child is heart-wrenching. Yet emotions cannot lead the way when a life-or-death decision is on the line. When we search for scientific data about CDH rather than simply relying on what an abortion provider tells us, we can find a more specific explanation of what it is: a condition in which the diaphragm—the muscle that separates the abdomen from the chest—does not develop completely, causing a hole where abdominal organs can migrate into the chest. When that happens, it doesn't leave enough space for the lungs to develop normally, making it hard for the baby to breathe. The severity of the condition depends on the size and position of the hernia. Additionally, treatment is possible, with a survival rate that can be greater than 90%, according to Johns Hopkins All Children's, which founded the first inpatient center in the country dedicated solely to the treatment of CDH.[2] Like ALL life-limiting conditions, every case of CDH is different and dependent on many different factors.

We share this example to point out how vital it is to research your child's condition by carefully reading and evaluating multiple sources, regardless of what you may have been told about your child's chances.

Find objective sources.

Keep in mind the importance of objective data as you search multiple sources. It seems unreasonable, for example, to expect an abortion provider to provide an unbiased opinion of the value of a baby with a life-limiting condition. On the other hand, it is also unrealistic to only read stories of children living and thriving with your child's condition, as encouraging and hopeful as that can be.

While I did say it was beyond the scope of this book to provide specific information about a number of diagnoses, I do think it is helpful to share one source that can help almost anyone reading this. Though I hesitate to share websites in general because of how quickly they can change, PubMed Central® is a free, full-text archive of biomedical and life sciences journal literature at the U.S. National Institutes of Health's National Library of Medicine. I have used this site to research a number of conditions, for my own benefit as the mother of a child with Trisomy 18 as well as for the benefit of the community we serve. If you can wade through scientific jargon, it is well worth your time and effort to focus at least some of your research here:

https://www.ncbi.nlm.nih.gov/pmc/

Sometimes simply reading the abstract will give you enough insight to answer your own questions (or calm your own fears). If you find you are needing to justify certain decisions regarding the life of your baby, perhaps to advocate for fair care, for example, then you may choose to print out entire articles to take to your medical team. This is definitely a source which commands respect from the medical community.

Other premier pediatric journals you can search include *Pediatrics*, *American Journal of Medical Genetics*, and *Pediatric Cardiology*.

If you're just not sure what to make of an article's conclusions, bring it to your next appointment and ask the doctor what it means. He or she should be able to cut through the medical jargon and explain it in everyday English!

Keep the big picture in mind.

If, in your research, you find you are overwhelmed by the sheer amount of information, or if it is just too difficult to make sense of all the scientific data when your emotions threaten to spill over, enlist some help. Can your spouse take on the role of researcher? Or maybe a close friend or relative? Don't feel **you** have to be the one doing all the work. Mama, it's hard enough just taking care of yourself and your sweet baby! If you are driven to find answers and find a certain amount of satisfaction in learning more, then by all means—go for it. But if it has the opposite effect, then please reach out for help.

Your child is not a diagnosis. Your sweet baby is not defined by this condition. Yes, it will shape that little life, just as it is already shaping your life. But in the grand scheme of all eternity, remember this. You don't have to know everything to give your baby what he or she needs most of all: your love.

Chapter 9
What If…

Every life represented on a gravestone has a dash—the time in between a person's life and death. God brings us into this life, and He brings us out. God's got our dash!

–Yvette

Before we get into the specifics of what your own medical team has discovered with relation to your child's specific condition, we need to look at the broader picture. Whether you have a confirmed diagnosis or only a suspicion, read this chapter carefully so you can consider possibilities that may not have entered your mind yet. It is our desire to provide as much information as possible. As difficult as it is to face the unknowns, it is even harder if you prepare for one outcome and find yourself unexpectedly dealing with something you hadn't even considered.

What if the diagnosis is wrong?

It is likely that if you've read this far, you have already received a definite diagnosis for your baby. But we would be remiss to overlook an important fact: it is entirely possible that a prenatal diagnosis is not 100% correct. While it is true that prenatal screening is more advanced than ever before, it is also true that technology can fail us on occasion. More than one mother can share a story of being told that her unborn child had a certain syndrome or abnormality only to give birth to a perfectly healthy child. With the rise of technology, these instances are certainly not as common these days; however, it is worth mentioning that sometimes testing misses the mark completely.

Abigail, a mother who experienced this, comments, "I was strongly pressured to abort my totally healthy daughter. Why? Well, that's a great question. The doctor who spent my entire appointment berating me said that there was a 'spot' on the ultrasound that could be a 'glitch' or could indicate Down Syndrome. He was obsessed with trying to convince me to abort her. He didn't want me to do further testing. Told me I needed to hurry. I was treated quite poorly after that, despite the fact that there was no medical indication for a diagnosis of Down Syndrome. It completely ruined my pregnancy because I felt helpless and feared for her life."

Abigail's experience reminds us how important it is to know the limits and parameters of prenatal tests, whether ultrasound or blood test or other type of screening. Noninvasive prenatal testing, sometimes known as NIPT or NIPS, is a blood test frequently done early in pregnancy. It analyzes small fragments of free-floating DNA from the placenta that are found along with the mother's own DNA in her blood. Since DNA from placental cells is usually identical to the baby's DNA, analyzing the DNA from the placenta allows for a look at the genetic make-up of the baby without potentially causing harm to the unborn child (hence the term *noninvasive*). However, this method is only a *screening*, which means it does not give a definitive answer as to whether a child does or does not have a particular genetic condition. The test only estimates whether the risk for certain conditions is increased or decreased. And because it examines both mother's and baby's DNA, the test can also pick up on a genetic condition of the mother rather than the baby.

Noninvasive prenatal testing is ***not*** a diagnostic tool. NIPT alone can give both false negative and false positive results. However, this can often be the basis of a provider's pressure for further testing, such as an amniocentesis, which is a method of collecting genetic material from amniotic fluid and has its own risks. Not all mothers choose an amniocentesis for various reasons, but some feel pressured to get the diagnostic test to confirm whether or not the baby has the indicated genetic condition. Even worse, NIPT results can also be the basis for a push toward abortion.

Julie speaks to this potential confusion as she shares her experience. "The genetic counselor initiated the conversation of abortion at the same time she delivered my NIPT results. This haunts me. I wonder how many younger mothers (more likely to have a false positive NIPT) choose to terminate their pregnancies, not realizing that bloodwork is not a diagnosis. The maternal fetal specialist also advised me to terminate the pregnancy for three visits in a row. Each visit, we informed her that we wanted to give Sophia a chance. She finally honored our decision and ceased recommending abortion."

You may be reading through this book having only received the suspicious findings of a blood test or ultrasound rather than a confirmed diagnosis—and that's okay. Whether or not you choose to find out "for sure" about your baby's condition is entirely up to you, and in fact, we'll take a look at the pros and cons of receiving a confirmed prenatal diagnosis momentarily. If you are unsure of whether to go forward with further testing, we would encourage you to pray, gather information, talk to trusted professionals, and feel at peace with whatever you decide. Many people opt to forego more testing, saying it wouldn't make a difference as to whether they continue the pregnancy anyway, so why increase the risk? Others simply desire to know for sure in order to research and prepare for what the future might bring. Either way, you are here gathering as much information as you can, preparing yourself to be the best mother or father for your special baby as possible, and we applaud and encourage you on this journey.

What if a prenatal diagnosis is actually a drawback?

For better or for worse, anomalies or defects that in the past would have remained hidden while the mother continued the pregnancy in blissful ignorance of potential problems are now put in the spotlight and scrutinized. This can be helpful in seeking treatments and preparing birth and care plans, as we will discuss in the next section of the book. Yet, ironically, these advances can also bring about self-fulfilling prophecies.

When I was researching while pregnant with Verity, I found a medical article with a stunning conclusion regarding the outcomes for babies with Trisomy 13 or 18:

The single most important factor independently related to mortality before going home or before one year, even when correcting for all other factors (including congenital anomalies, interventions, and palliative care), was the presence of a prenatal diagnosis.[1]

The vast differences in outcomes and care plans for children with a prenatal vs. a postnatal diagnosis showed up in several ways. For those who had a prenatal diagnosis, the study found that parents have similar hopes: they desire to meet their child alive, take their child home, be a family, and give their child the best life possible. (Perhaps these hopes are in line with your own.) So what did medical providers recommend to these parents whose hopes are outlined thus? According to the study, medical professionals all recommended that the parents choose comfort care at birth, with no intention of prolonging life. Referring to other medical articles and resources, the authors of this study noted that these recommendations were probably based solely on the chromosomal diagnosis, as evidenced by many position statements, hospital policies, and authors who consider interventions for these conditions to be "futile."[2]

Postnatal diagnoses for the respondents in the study came an average of six days after birth. This means any interventions came as a result of medical personnel doing their jobs, noting the needs of the babies and acting accordingly. For example, babies who did not have a genetic diagnosis prior to birth received ventilator support based on their respiratory needs.

There was even a marked distinction between what was considered "palliative care" for babies with a prenatal vs. postnatal diagnosis. (This term, by the way, can have vastly different nuances depending on where the care is given. We will explore types of post-birth care in the next chapter of this book.) According to the study, the parents of children with a prenatal diagnosis of trisomy 13 or 18 were directed toward a palliative care plan with a goal seemingly to give the child an "optimal death." However, for children whose diagnosis did not come until after delivery, palliative care consisted of such interventions as tube feedings, surgeries, respiratory support, and even heart surgery.[3] (For the record, many doctors would not consider these interventions "palliative!")

Sadly, a prenatal diagnosis can be a potential pitfall to receiving fair care. Unfortunately, there are many documented cases of children being denied basic life-saving measures simply on the basis of their genetic condition. According to Bridget Mora,

Parents who receive a serious prenatal or neonatal diagnosis are often told that their baby's disabilities are "incompatible with life" or that the baby has a "fatal fetal

anomaly." The label "incompatible with life" often reflects a physician's judgment of quality of life, not an actual medical diagnosis. Whatever the intention of the individual using it, the language dehumanizes the baby and may encourage abortion or the withdrawal of life-sustaining care…. "Incompatible with life" becomes a self-fulfilling prophecy when parents carry their baby to term and treatments offered to other babies are withheld from theirs. It simply is not known at this point what the survival rate would be for babies with trisomy 13 and 18 if medically indicated treatments were fully considered in each case.[4]

These are sobering facts, but if you have received a definite prenatal diagnosis, having an awareness of the potential pitfalls can prepare you to advocate more specifically for your baby. Take heart! Knowledge is power, and you are doing the hard work of gathering and sorting information that will help you in the days and weeks to come.

What if the diagnosis is worse than reality?

Even in instances when there is absolute certainty of a genetic condition, the severity of the condition or its related complications can often be either over or understated, depending on what exactly can be determined through further evaluations and screenings. Holes in hearts may close on their own, making surgery unnecessary after all. Enlarged kidneys may return to a normal size, projecting the ability to function normally. A condition that at first seems to present as life-threatening may change during the natural course of pregnancy to the point where a simple procedure will provide what is necessary to sustain life after birth.

Vanessa only had a suspicion during her pregnancy that her son Fernando had Trisomy 18, a suspicion that quickly turned to her new reality when Fernando was born with a low birth weight and several obvious physical anomalies. Vanessa remembers the moment the chief geneticist confirmed Fernando's diagnosis: "At that moment, his fight and my fight began. The doctors wanted me to take him home, love him, no medicine or interventions, just keep him comfortable until he died. I trusted those doctors. Why wouldn't I? They knew more than me about medicine, about babies, about breathing, about dying....Every day I was told he had a few hours, then a few days. Then Fernando took over and taught me that his time here was not going to be dictated by what doctors assumed about him! I followed my son's lead. I learned as much as I could about medical equipment, diagnoses, medical care, and I took it day by day, month by month, year by year."

Fernando lived a beautiful life with his parents and older brother Giancarlo, going to heaven shortly before his fourth birthday. He touched many lives and continues to inspire others—far surpassing the expectations of doctors who encouraged his mother to just keep him comfortable until he died.

Gabriela resisted her physician's efforts to convince her to abort her son Gabriel after receiving a prenatal diagnosis. She writes, "While it was unknown if little Gabriel would make it to or beyond birth, we prepared to welcome him into our family with as much love and care as possible, taking joy in the gift of his life and preparing a detailed birth plan with full interventions."

Gabriel entered the world a week ahead of his mama's scheduled C-section. With some unexpected complications during the birthing process, he was not breathing on his own at first, so they intubated him and transported him to the NICU. Gabriela recalls the next three months being full of "tumultuous ups and downs and many near death experiences before coming home one day shy of three months old with a trach, feeding tube, and more." Gabriel does have some medical complications and considerations for daily life. However, despite all of this, his mother says, "He is a happy and sweet little guy who loves being held and kissed, going outdoors and lounging in the jacuzzi. He has enriched the lives of all who know him, including his many fans online. He is breathtakingly handsome with his long eyelashes, doll-like face and beautiful wavy brown hair. He is loved beyond measure."

Having been part of the rare trisomy community for some years now, I can attest to many other stories like these—parents who were told their child would not make it to birth, or if so, they should keep their expectations low. Yet I know many living, thriving children who enrich the lives of their families and communities because the parents chose to let their babies lead the way, giving them the opportunity to defy statistics and write their own stories.

Every mother who faces a life-limiting diagnosis for her baby deserves the opportunity to see her child's story unfold. Whether that story has dozens of chapters or only a few—it is a story worth telling, because GOD is the author, and He has eternal purposes written on every page.

What if reality is worse than the diagnosis?

Lest we paint too rosy of a picture, we must acknowledge things can go the other way as well. Ultrasounds and fetal echocardiograms can only give us so much information while the baby is *in utero*. While there are many happy stories of a baby's condition at birth not being nearly as dire as predicted, we also know of heartbreakingly difficult situations in which no one could have possibly known the extent of the baby's condition.

Dawn, mother of baby Athena, experienced the ultimate grief of birthing her precious baby only to have to say goodbye a mere 17 hours later. Unbeknownst to Dawn and her medical team, Athena had many internal complications that did not show up on the prenatal scans. While the parents and medical team were prepared to give Athena life-saving interventions at birth based on what they did know in advance, the reality was much worse than anyone had anticipated.

Dawn shares, "I'd been so focused on interventions and children thriving that I was not prepared for losing her at all. I thought I'd be bringing her home alive. We're always told in the support groups that things may look different after birth than what they look like on the scan—that certain problems spotted may not actually be there. Well, in Athy's case, an array of serious defects were missed on her scans. The extra chromosome had inflicted that much damage; she was never going to survive. I think we need as a whole community to prepare women more for this. Sometimes, no intervention will be enough, and child loss is an inevitable reality for many who choose to go to term. Sometimes, no matter how hard we advocate, no matter what interventions, it won't change the outcome."

As much as I'd love to guarantee that everyone choosing to carry these precious babies to term will be able to take them home and love them for years to come, the reality is that statistics are there for a reason. A life-limiting diagnosis is just that—a diagnosis that, based on numbers alone, indicates a child's life is limited in some way, whether by the conditions he or she will face just trying to breathe and eat or whether by the number of days or even hours which he or she will live before passing on. It hurts to think about it. Yet ignoring the full range of possibilities does a disservice to parents.

It is our vision that someday, all medical professionals will share stories of hope and encouragement with mothers and fathers who receive a prenatal diagnosis. Some do, of course, but many push their clients toward abortion or toward preparing only for a baby to die an early death. At the same time, it is an unfortunate reality that many parents do not experience the joy of bringing their baby home from the hospital alive. We have to acknowledge the uncertainty of any outcome. And even when our children are born alive and come home, there is never a guarantee of how long they might be with us.

As Hannah said, “Interventions help our kids thrive, but it will not make them invincible.” Hannah’s Evelyn (whose story is featured in the first chapter) overcame many odds with a plethora of surgeries and interventions. She lived an amazing 3 ½ years and continues to bless others with her legacy as her parents carry out the mission of their nonprofit, Evelyn’s Treehouse. Yet even with medical support, those interventions could only carry Evelyn so far.

Dawn and Hannah are part of a large community of bereaved parents of medically complex children who are thankful for the time they had with their precious children, despite the immense pain of letting them go. Be encouraged that even if this is the path laid out before you, it is possible to find peace and beauty in the journey amidst the grief and heartache of loss.

Even though Dawn’s experience was not what she had envisioned, she wants other parents to know something: “As much as I was not emotionally ready or prepared for how fast I lost Athy, I would not change a thing. We sang to her and told her stories and had her blessed and stroked her. And when they eventually handed her to me, she looked directly into my eyes. A deep knowing passed between us. I will remember that moment for the rest of my life. Every bit of pain I feel is all love for her, and worth it for that moment alone. I pray it was all worth it for Athena, too.”

What if…what if…what if…

We’ve covered some important “what ifs” when it comes to a prenatal diagnosis. The truth is, you’ll be pondering your own list of “what ifs” for what will seem like a very long time. Add them to your growing list of notes and questions and address them when you can while understanding that there are no easy answers.

Continue educating yourself while maintaining a healthy relationship with your research—don't let it take over your life! Take a break to do something that brings you joy, and make your mental and emotional health a priority during this time.

Most of all, determine now to be intentional with your decisions and to explore every avenue within the realm of possibility, not only for your baby, but also for yourself. No matter what is on your particular path, you will likely face lingering questions about what might have been. Give yourself the grace to release those questions, freeing yourself from regrets both now and in the future. You are doing the best you can with what you have and what you know. And that, dear one, is more than enough. You are exactly the right person to care for your baby!

Chapter 10

What Does Your Medical Team Say?

It's OK to switch doctors, caregivers, hospitals, etc. Don't settle for a doctor that doesn't agree with the way you want to move forward. The good medical teams want to learn and listen to their patients.
–Selina

The level of support you may receive from your own doctors depends on many factors. It is difficult to speak in broad terms about this. Parents' experiences with their medical teams have ranged from completely supportive and willing to give any life-saving interventions necessary at birth to completely resistant, refusing to continue seeing the mother, constantly pushing for an abortion, or denying the possibility of giving needed interventions.

As you ask questions, have discussions, and continue your research, you will find yourself developing your own ideas and opinions of what you desire your delivery experience to be as well as the care for your baby at birth. This leads to an essential next step—creating your birth plan—which we will cover in a later chapter. But keep it in mind, because all your appointments during pregnancy will give you important pieces of the puzzle that ultimately you and God will assemble.

Here are some considerations to keep in mind as you have these important conversations with your medical providers.

Location matters.

There is a term in the rare trisomy community: *trisomy-friendly hospital.* As mentioned in the research shared in the previous chapter, sometimes having a prenatal diagnosis means a mother and baby will face a certain level of discrimination when it comes to life-supporting care. And it's not always the baby who is denied surgical interventions. Some doctors refuse to perform a C-section for a mother whose child they don't expect to survive anyway. Whether or not you personally will need a C-section to deliver your baby isn't the point. It's the attitude behind the decision. This is why you must have frank conversations with your medical team to address the range of possibilities that lie before you and ensure everyone is on the same page when it comes to caring for both mother and child. If you feel uncomfortable with the answers you are receiving to your questions or with the attitudes and assumptions you sense are behind the assertions of your care team, then it may be best to part ways and find another provider that will be better aligned with your needs and desires.

Take someone along with you to your appointments.

Most of us find "thinking on our feet" a difficult task when we are experiencing such a mentally and emotionally taxing journey. It's not uncommon to forget all your questions once you're sitting in the exam room or to feel you've lost access to even the most basic vocabulary after hearing some unexpected news. If it is at all possible, take someone along with you to your appointments. This person should know what your desires and preferences are, be comfortable asking questions on your behalf, and take copious notes so you can sort through information at a later time. Perhaps your spouse will easily take on this role. Or maybe you can ask a trusted friend or another close family member. But don't be afraid to ask someone to help you in this way! It's also an opportunity for someone who loves you to do something tangible to help on this journey.

Know what level of care you want for your baby and communicate your desires.

Three terms are often used interchangeably when it comes to the level of care for a person with a life-limiting diagnosis. Let's get a basic foundation laid for *comfort care, hospice care,* and *palliative care* while at the same time recognizing the true meaning of these types of care—as in how they are practically implemented—varies greatly depending on your location.

Comfort care—When the medical team uses this phrase, they are trying to say there is really nothing that can be done to help the patient long term. The goal is to keep the patient comfortable, relieve any suffering, and ease his or her passing. The focus is on caring rather than curing.

Hospice care—This level of care is for people in the dying process. While we typically think of hospice care as being at home, it can also be found in other locations, although this may not be relevant since we are speaking of a baby rather than an elderly client. Hospice care provides visits from medical and spiritual care team members as well as any needed medications and medical equipment.

Palliative care—Viki Kind of Kind Ethics describes it this way: "It describes both pain management when you're healthy and the support you receive during the dying process. Palliative care is the global word to describe all of the care that is related to relieving suffering."[1] As you see from this definition, palliative care can overlap with comfort or hospice care.

I will say it again: the working definitions of these types of care vary considerably from place to place, so it's important your discussions with your care team include specifics that will help you understand exactly what a doctor means when he or she refers to "comfort care" or "palliative care."

For example, is a feeding tube allowed with comfort care? Supplemental oxygen? The answers could be *yes* or *no*, depending on where you are. And based on the answers, you will then need to determine if they line up with what YOU want for your baby. This leads to our next point of consideration.

What types of interventions are you comfortable with providing for your baby if needed?

Since comfort, hospice, and palliative care can be such nebulous terms, it may be easier to decide what interventions you desire your baby to receive if needed and then determine with your medical team how that matches up with their classifications. (Depending on where you are delivering, you may not even need to label what type of care you are requesting. We did not have to do this. Other parents, however, report that their care teams ask this question specifically so they can be prepared at delivery to meet the requests and requirements of both Mom and Baby.)

Let's review some possible interventions with a description of them. Please note this is not an exhaustive list, and as this chapter's title notes, you should be discussing all of this with your medical team, who can provide more specifics and answer your questions. Also, please note the following discussion is intended to be an objective description of some common types of interventions. Whether they are appropriate for your baby's unique situation is up to you and your medical team to discuss and decide. (Keep in mind your decisions may change as you receive further information about your baby's condition.)

Feeding support. Usually an NG (nasogastric) or OG (orogastric) tube will be given to a neonate so that breast milk or formula can be passed through the nasal or oral passageway to the stomach. This can be a temporary solution which a baby can outgrow, or perhaps the child will continue to need help receiving nutrition long term. In this case, the parents and care team may opt for a surgical placement of a feeding tube. The more commonly used gastrostomy tube (G-tube) delivers food directly into the stomach, while the jejunostomy tube (J-tube) is inserted into the middle part of the small intestine. Many children who start their lives needing feeding tubes can go on to "graduate" to oral eating (if conditions are safe for them to do so) with feeding or occupational therapy and a lot of persistence. Other children live happy, comfortable lives receiving all or most of their nutrition via feeding tube, receiving oral tastes as tolerated for exploration and pleasure.

Parents receive training so they know exactly what to do for their babies and how to do it. They will become familiar with all necessary equipment and be connected with a medical supply company. Dietitians provide information and support, as do gastroenterologists. If surgery is needed and chosen, parents will consult with the surgeon ahead of time. For mothers who desire to give their babies breast milk, lactation consultants can help arrange for breast pumps and supplies. While it is indeed overwhelming to consider all of these things, remember that anything new takes time to learn.

Breathing support. This one is extremely important, as respiratory issues are often the cause of early death, which is one reason doctors try to keep babies *in utero* as long as possible unless there are complications compromising the health of Mom and/or Baby. It is not unusual for babies with a life-limiting diagnosis to need help with breathing right after birth. A bit of oxygen via nasal cannula may be enough to keep the blood oxygen saturations at healthy levels. Or perhaps CPAP (continuous positive airway pressure) will be needed for a short while before stepping down to a cannula. In more serious cases, the situation may call for intubation. This is inserting a tube through the baby's mouth into his or her airway and using a ventilator to push air into the lungs. As with the feeding tube, any kind of breathing interventions may be temporary, allowing the baby time to grow enough to breathe without any devices. Or perhaps the child only needs breathing assistance during sleeping or traveling. In some cases, a child may need a tracheostomy, a surgery to provide a tube in the airway to keep it open for breathing. Some children eventually "graduate" from the trach, with their airway opening enough to not need the additional breathing support. Other children continue needing this life-saving intervention.

As mentioned in the previous section, parents receive training and support so they can help their babies with any interventions that they need in order to come home. While this likely feels scary to think about, many families have respiratory support equipment at home, from oxygen tanks and concentrators to ventilators and suctioning machines. Your child's pulmonologist and otolaryngologist (ear, nose, and throat doctor) will help you understand your child's unique situation and what can be done to support it.

Life support. Cardiopulmonary resuscitation (CPR) can be performed on infants if they stop breathing or if their heart stops beating. Compressing and ventilating may help bring a baby back over the threshold and give him or her another chance at life. If such action is needed, are you willing to request it, and is your medical team willing to provide it? If so, it's important to be proactive in assigning your baby full code status and making sure everyone knows about it. Heartbreaking situations have happened when a DNR (do not resuscitate) order is placed on a child without the parents' knowledge or consent. If you desire for your baby to receive life-saving interventions no matter what his or her diagnosis, make it known that your baby is FULL CODE.

Cardiac support. Heart problems can be a stand-alone issue or one of multiple difficulties associated with a particular genetic condition. An echocardiogram shortly after birth can confirm the absence or presence of anomalies as well as their severity. The good news is that cardiac issues are rarely something that need attention immediately after birth. There is usually time to stabilize and assess the baby, determining exactly what the complications are, and make a plan for treatment. However, heart surgery is one area where the issue of "fair care" can surface. Often surgeries that would be performed without question on "normal" children are denied to those who have a life-limiting condition—*even though surgery could remove some of those limitations!*

Parents should attend to the most pressing needs of their baby at birth. When cardiac issues are present, there should be time to gather information, consult with specialists, and then make your decisions regarding cardiac interventions.

Non-life-threatening support. A number of conditions or anomalies may be present that do not threaten the life of your baby. However, as you consider his or her quality of life, you may choose to provide interventions that can help your child in the long term. Examples include clubfoot casting, surgery to remove an extra thumb, corrective splints, and cleft palate repair. These measures can usually wait, but they are steps to consider if or when you bring your baby home from the hospital and settle into your own routine.

It's all right to change your mind!

As you look over all these options and possibilities, you may have strong opinions about certain interventions and what you desire your baby's care to look like. But we would be remiss to neglect an important consideration: many families change their plans along the journey!

Rhonda, mother to Bella Grace and founder of The Bella Grace Foundation, remembers, "I was almost afraid at first to tell them I changed my mind from comfort care to giving interventions. They received it well and weren't surprised. I feel that along the journey, especially prenatally, you meet with so many different people with differing opinions wanting you to make decisions based on a baby you've only seen on a TV screen. The best words I heard after I told them I wanted to fight for Bella Grace when she came were, 'We will let her take the lead and tell us what she needs; she will write her own story.' It was such a relief."

This change of mind is not uncommon. Researchers Janvier, Farlow, and Barrington discovered in the rare trisomy experience, "Decisions were influenced by the state of the child and whether he was vigorous or weak, with parents in general not wanting to impose undue suffering. Parents of almost half the children discharged on comfort care later decided to consider surgical interventions, because their child exceeded expectations (p. 7)."[2]

On the other hand, as we discussed in the last chapter, sometimes a change in plans can go the opposite direction. When the baby's condition is considerably more severe than expected, parents may be faced with having to relinquish fighting a battle that can't be won. It is heartbreakingly difficult to come to a point where you feel doing what is best for your child involves ***not*** offering the interventions you originally planned, but hear this: sometimes it is the BEST option for a child.

Bottom line? Make plans…but hold them loosely. Allow space (and grace) to implement changes as you receive new information. Communicate with your medical team your desires and preferences, but also make it clear that you reserve the right to change your mind along the way.

You are here reading this book because you love your sweet baby. Mama, Dad—YOU are the expert on your child. No one else can make these difficult decisions for you. I wish we could give you answers, tell you what to do in this situation or that. But no one else can (or should) speak in absolute terms when it comes to situations like this. I believe decisions made from a heart of love will be guided by wisdom. Learn all you can, plan as best as possible, but give yourself plenty of grace, both now and after making a decision. And if anyone makes you feel bad about what you choose for YOUR baby, then draw a boundary line and audit them out of your inner circle!

Mary's story

We've looked at some clinical information, so before we get to a list of questions you may wish to take to your medical team, I'd like to share a personal story that brings home just how difficult and delicate this whole process can be.

A mutual friend connected me with Mary soon after we received Verity's diagnosis. Mary had walked a similar journey with her sweet Moriah Joy just the year before we met online. Though her grief at losing Moriah was still fresh, Mary kindly reached out to me, sharing frankly what she had learned and experienced through her pregnancy, delivery, and all-too-brief time at home with her precious baby. Mary's raw honesty reached me in my darkest time of grieving over Verity's diagnosis, and the connections she helped me make with other members of the rare trisomy community became our lifeline. Additionally, the lingering questions Mary had about her own experience provided insight I could never have gleaned in all my research.

Mary and I have remained in touch over the years, and she has graciously agreed to let me share her story here in hopes it will help other families on this difficult journey. Mary and her husband brought Moriah home before she was 24 hours old and had her for seven days. Here are the words she shared with me in the fall of 2016.

What I wish I HAD known was that I had the power to speak up. To be bold in my thoughts and questions and to say what I thought felt right. [My husband] thought we were on the same page in that meeting, but I didn't speak up what my Momma's heart was screaming...I thought I was just being emotional. Basically, we were told about the option for "Comfort Care." And as I asked questions regarding other care, like for her heart, or for breathing, or for feeding, I was told that if I asked for help for one thing it would SNOWBALL to my baby being on a life-sustaining machine.

I left so discouraged. I found that on one hand, the doctors were saying there was absolutely no way to say if my baby would take a breath or that her heart would remember to keep beating after birth. But at the same time, they were telling me that I should sign up for comfort care, which means there is absolutely no intervention and only what the child can do on their own is done. If the baby can't breathe properly, their heart doesn't beat properly, they can't feed properly...then that is how it is.

But! Wait! There HAS to be something MORE, my heart was screaming inside. There HAS to be an in-between! I found that every person has a different opinion on what is "quality of life." Even my husband and I are different. The doctor said things like, the baby will be in pain if you give it a feeding tube, or a ventilator, and that the quality of life for them just would not be good. What I wish I had known is that there ARE other options in between. But in all of this, there is the weird balance of trusting Jesus hears you and knows best and IS in control. But also wondering where do we step in honor the life He has given us to cherish and protect in a world that does not know Him?

We did say "Comfort Care—with exceptions." For me, it is my biggest regret. An example, when Moriah was born: she was ALIVE! She was trying to BREATHE! She was trying, but she couldn't, because [her airway] was blocked. She needed help to suction it out! I have it on video. I said, "I think she needs help! She has something in her throat, help her!" And again, "Help her!" Then my husband yells at them to get the aspirator bulb. They give it him, and he does his best to help, and indeed she breathes and cries! But why—why did the doctor not help with something so simple?! Why did she keep telling us over and over in those moments, "We expected this, she may not breathe, it's just how it may be..."

Not all doctors will be this way. I don't know if she had ever helped deliver a baby like Moriah. I wonder too if her training and education caused her to also be fearful of this moment and she was guarding her own heart and emotions from what could be.

When I look back, I think there could have been options for Moriah's heart rate. Others said caffeine can be used for low heart rate. That option was never presented, though it sounds like it would have been a simple and painless intervention to try. Moriah had multiple apnea episodes in the hospital. I had read about families who dealt with apnea for months. But we weren't really told anything about it. There are different kinds. We were never told about what type she had. Moriah's color was not good, especially after the apnea episodes. She always had labored breathing and low heart rate, but oxygen was never offered. Even just to try! In all this, I don't wish that Moriah was healed and perfect, or that the medical professionals "fixed" her, but that at least she could have been comfortable rather than laboring so hard.

You just don't know until your baby is here and you see her strengths and weaknesses in live action. But I would say be open to trying options, and closing them if need be, when you know they aren't necessary or helpful.

Nearly five years after sharing the above story with me, Mary adds this thought, "Moriah Joy means 'The Lord will provide joy.' It took time until I felt like that was true for me. But it is!"

Suggested questions to ask your medical team

In light of all that we have discussed thus far, we offer the following list of generic questions that can perhaps start the conversation with your medical team. We encourage you to add to this list based on your child's unique needs. Don't be afraid to speak up and speak out. YOU are the parent of your child. He or she is ultimately YOUR responsibility. While you may feel overwhelmed and underprepared to make difficult decisions, be assured that there are resources and help available. The more you research, the more questions you ask, the more you interact with other parents, the better equipped you will be for this momentous task of caring for your special baby.

- What experience do you have with this diagnosis? Have you personally delivered/cared for a mother/baby with this same diagnosis?
- What exactly do we KNOW about our baby's condition? What is NOT KNOWN but needs to be assessed and possibly addressed at birth?

- Are you willing to perform a C-section if it's necessary in order for us to meet the baby alive?
- Where will the delivery be? Does the location have a NICU prepared for the needs our baby may have? (Depending on potential complications, you may want to request a level 4 NICU.)
- Will you support giving life-saving interventions to our baby as needed? (Treat the baby, not the diagnosis?)
- If at a hospital that doesn't offer certain surgeries—what surrounding hospitals do you work with and generally transfer patients to?
- Do you have a complex care team?
- What does palliative care look like in this facility? Is there a palliative care team? If so, can we schedule a meeting?
- Based on our baby's known condition, what do you anticipate the needs to be at birth?
- Will a parent be able to stay with the baby? Or are there lodging options (Ronald McDonald House, etc.) we should investigate?
- In the event our baby passes before or soon after birth, what resources are available for families? What are the typical protocols for such an event? Do we have the option to use a Cuddle Cot (see chapter 15)?

Chapter 11
What Do Real People Say?

Take it one second, hour, day at a time. NO ONE is guaranteed the next second, hour, or day so try to not overthink things and enjoy the now. God is in control. These babies are huge blessings…every life has purpose.

–Kristen

Looking at research and listening to medical experts are actions in this quest to broaden awareness and educate yourself on your child's condition. An important third component, though, is to get a little more personal. While research and statistics can be helpful, real-life stories bring the heart and soul of your experience into crystal clarity. Raw data can only take you so far. Real descriptions, on the other hand, enhance your learning adventure and bring the abstract into the realm of personal, individual experience.

Find your tribe.

No matter how rare your child's diagnosis, it's likely there are specific support groups for families living out the day-to-day reality associated with that particular diagnosis. If you haven't already been provided with any links or resources to these types of groups, please search! My husband and I spent a very fear-filled, lonely month after learning about Verity's condition before we realized there were other children living and thriving with Trisomy 18. Not only that, but when I learned we could find community with others on the journey regardless of what happened with our particular story, I literally cried tears of joy.

As a side note, it is entirely possible that you may encounter difficulty finding a group related to your child's diagnosis, especially if it is the one-in-a-million type of diagnosis. If this is the case for you, try searching for groups specifically supporting parents who receive a life-limiting diagnosis for their babies. If you haven't already found our private support group, you are welcome to join us![1]

The online support groups we finally found were a lifeline to our souls. We were not alone after all! We now had a new community, a new tribe, who welcomed us with open arms. I remember sentiments such as, "Welcome to the club you never wanted to join. We are here for you. We've all been there, heartbroken and terrified. You can do this, and we will help you." I posted questions. I followed blogs from other families written about their little ones. I was amazed to find pictures and videos of living, laughing babies and children—CHILDREN! I had been told our daughter would likely not make it to her first birthday, and I was astonished to see children and even teens and adults living with the same condition as Verity.

The support groups didn't sugar-coat this life. Nor did they hide the difficult times. Babies and children passed away. I cried and cried over these precious souls I had never met in person, aching for their parents and imagining how it would be when it was our turn. I saw other parents posting difficult questions, with a range of replies that helped me understand not every question has easy or definite answers. "It depends…" was the start of many responses.

Seeing the good, the bad, and the ugly in the months leading up to our due date prepared us mentally and emotionally in a way that wouldn't have happened if we had not been introduced to these families. It didn't matter that we wouldn't meet any of them in person until months or even years later—technology gave us the precious gift of connection.

If you haven't already done so, ***find your tribe!*** You'll be so thankful you did.

Listen and learn with discernment…and a grain of salt.

As much as I highly recommend finding and joining appropriate online support groups, let me speak a few words of caution here. Some of us have learned the following points the hard way.

1. *Not everyone believes or thinks the same as you.* Often our hearts get connected quickly because we are so excited and grateful to have found others who "get it." Be careful of assuming you know someone's perspective and story. Until or unless you have the opportunity to deeply connect, not just online but perhaps via chatting or even meeting in person, you probably don't truly ***know*** that other person.

2. *Not all contacts in a support group are in a healthy place themselves.* People's comments and reactions may be coming from a place of deep pain, so they may say something that seems jarring or hurtful to others. Perhaps there is implied judgment for other parents' decisions or outright hostility when a "wrong" course of action is described. There have even been instances of families

getting scammed by a parent who was supposedly in a similar situation. (That is rare, and yet it's a real thing—people pretending to have a medically fragile child in order to gain sympathy and donations.) Be cautious, wise, and discerning in your interactions. Don't be afraid to "unfriend" or block someone who is causing mental and emotional stress. And remember—you don't have to accept friend requests or follow people just because their child has the same diagnosis as yours.

3. *The same diagnosis does not mean the same outcome.* I looked for similarities in other stories I read in our groups, yearning for any insight to help me know what to expect with Verity. My hopes rose and fell as little ones survived and succeeded or met with an early end. This was unhealthy for me mentally and emotionally. I had to come to terms with NOT knowing or predicting anything. Verity had to be allowed to write her own story. She was not Rowan or Kayleigh or Orchid or any other little girl with Trisomy 18. While I could follow, learn from, and appreciate other families' experiences, I had to learn not to conflate their stories with the one God was writing for our family.

Don't be afraid to reach out.

Don't throw out the idea of having close personal friendships with people you've only met online just because they're online. Some of my most treasured connections came through me stepping out of my comfort zone to ask personal questions and carry on a conversation through private chat.

I noticed you're in Nebraska. Our baby will be delivered at UNMC. Are you close by?

I see you have a large homeschooling family, too! How do you do it all while caring for your T18 daughter?

I just wanted to thank you for sharing your blog. Your writing is so raw and beautiful. Thank you for sharing the good AND the bad parts of your journey.

Most parents in these types of support groups truly enjoy helping others along the way. We've all been on the other side, desperately seeking answers and feeling lost. While you may not connect as closely with some as with others, if someone seems to have had an experience similar to yours, if someone's answers demonstrate similar spiritual beliefs, or if someone simply writes something that resonates with you—reach out! If nothing else, your words may encourage someone else! And you may very well find yourself building a friendship that will last for years to come.

Learn from as many other parents as possible.

As we've alluded to before, you may face situations for which there are no easy answers. Listening to and learning from other parents who have "been there, done that" is so helpful when it comes to making decisions, for example, when it comes to certain interventions. You can also glean information and wisdom from other families' routines and life hacks. Use the search feature in support groups to seek out previous posts or questions similar to yours—sometimes comments from several years back may speak to where you are at currently. Parents in these support groups are so patient and willing to answer questions! And everyone has a different experience to share, so don't hesitate to ask a question just because it has been asked before. These groups are a place to learn from others on a continual basis.

We could fill another book with stories from real parents who have gone through a pregnancy wondering if their baby would make it to term, who have navigated NICU life, who use every kind of medical machine imaginable. It would be impossible to address every single issue in this one chapter, but perhaps the following insights from other parents who are a bit ahead of you in the journey will be encouraging to you. And perhaps they will spur you on to find your tribe (if you haven't already) and get involved.

The following quotes are from parents in the online support groups From Diagnosis to Delivery (a prenatal support group for parents who receive any kind of life-limiting diagnosis) and Rare Trisomy Parents (a parent-led group for families of children with a rare trisomy, some of whom are living and some of whom have passed). These parents hail from all over the United States as well as other countries around the world.

Receiving the diagnosis

After receiving Aaron's diagnosis, I thought the most terrifying thing would be to lose him. For us to continue with the pregnancy, for him to be stillborn or pass away in the following days. How could we do this, how could we let ourselves love? Then we found the From Diagnosis to Delivery support group and other parents who helped educate, navigate and encourage us. During the second half of our pregnancy and during Aaron's short six days of life, he taught us so much about hope, strength, faith, unconditional love and how to appreciate every moment of life regardless of your circumstances. We were so blessed to have had Aaron in our lives, even if it was so short. We are forever changed by his love and the love and support we found. If you are just starting your journey, know that you are not alone. –Jade

When I found out about my son's diagnosis, it changed me. I knew that God had set us on a journey that we never expected or even hoped to be on. But we were on it nonetheless. I quickly dove into research and trying to connect with other moms of children with the same diagnosis. We were quickly filled with hope at the prospect that—despite popular belief—it was possible that he could survive and maybe even thrive. We began pouring over stories of these fierce little fighters who were experiencing abundant life and joy despite having a life-limiting diagnosis. We read of families who had to say goodbye to their babies too soon but had such a peace about knowing they did the right thing, pursuing every possible intervention. –Rebekah

For a long time I was mad at Trisomy 18. I was angry, and I wanted to say that I hated it. But I knew that I had to love Trisomy 18 because it was part of who Everly was. So Everly has Trisomy 18. Period. That's part of who she is, and I love my daughter, therefore I love Trisomy 18. I may not love the things it does to her, but I do love her. –Jennie

As painful as the news may be, try to enjoy the journey. Every day is a blessing and time together. You will make it through things you don't think you can. –Nicole

Changing perspective

Fernando and his Trisomy 18 diagnosis brought to our lives a lot of fear, sacrifice, weakness and sadness; but most of all it has taught me how to be brave in the middle of weakness and fear. I have learned how sacrifice always ends in the biggest rewards, and how sadness quickly turns into happiness just by watching life through my son's eyes. All these feelings lead you to the greatest LOVE on earth, so how can we be scared of finding that type of love? –Vanessa

Yes, my daughter had Trisomy 13. But her diagnosis did not define who she was. When she was alive, she was so full of life, and so full of love. Trisomy 13 is a heartbreaking diagnosis.

But, these children are capable of having beautiful lives and being happy in their own little, perfect bubble. –Jessequine

You may not have the "perfect" or the "normal" baby you were expecting, and it is going to be a rollercoaster of emotions, but trust me when I say these babies bring love, strength and a fighting spirit like you have never seen before. They certainly teach us a lot and give you a new appreciation for life. However long your journey with this baby, even through pregnancy, just make every day count. You will never regret having an extra special baby. –Deborah

At the beginning I was so overwhelmed by the weight of my daughter's diagnosis. I felt like all the doctors had to tell me was worst-case scenario, and the doctors all came in very somber and sad, like she was already gone. Maebry is a fighter and has proven the doctors wrong time and time again. Yes, there are hard times and they are hard, but then she smiles at me and gets better and starts doing things I was told she was never supposed to do. It's all worth it! These kiddos are amazing. –Heidi

Family dynamics: Marriage

Shortly after I got Elisabeth's diagnosis, a Trisomy family told me that their son saved their marriage and healed their family. It was so different from what the neonatal team told us. They (neonatal nurse practitioner and team) said if I chose to go full term rather than induce labor right away, we'd end up divorced. A life-limiting diagnosis does put a lot of strain on a marriage. It's not easy. It takes a lot of work, but it's also an opportunity to become more vulnerable together and become closer as a couple than ever before. –Amy

I forgot to mention marriage…it will take a toll. You will be tired. It will seem overwhelming at first, but one thing this has taught me is that my husband isn't as verbal about his feelings as I am. I have to remember he is having a hard time too! He just won't say it as much as I do. I know it's hard, but try to remember your spouse wants your attention too. On this journey I think we forget about our marriage more often than we like to admit because our little kiddos demand our attention! Please redirect when your mind and heart allow you to. –Jayda

My biggest piece of advice as far as family dynamics is to practice lots and lots of grace. This all can be really hard, and there's no one right way to handle the tough emotions. –Paige

Family dynamics: Siblings

They told us from day one since we had other healthy kids at home, we should just sign a DNR [Do Not Resuscitate order] and let him pass in our arms because it would take so much time away from my other kids and cause them more harm than good. And my kids adore [our special-needs son] more than they have any other sibling. They all love to hold him and comfort him and hold his little hands. –Amanda

A [special-needs] child can positively affect his/her siblings. They learn compassion and kindness at a young age….When I was pregnant with Maristella, one of the reasons I was given to support termination was that she would have destroyed our family, our marriage, and that her siblings would have suffered because of her and would have been angry at her. Well, I believe that our family is BETTER because of Maristella!
–Raffaella

Do not fear for the siblings of children with disabilities, regardless if they are younger or older. The sibs have the rare opportunity to learn life lessons and skills that those in a "typical" household do not. Our sons have gained so many virtues because of their sister Ella Grace. I am not sure we could have ever taught them what Ella Grace has taught them. And children don't have these grand expectations. They will adapt and adjust easier than you think, so let them live. And yes, there will be sadness and possibly even loss, but that life experience is a blessing and a gift as well to the siblings. Our family cherishes the time we have together more than most families. I cannot imagine if we had not had Ella Grace to teach us about patience and God's love for us. –Maria

Interventions

One group of doctors told us we shouldn't intubate our child, because if we couldn't extubate her, we would feel like we were "pulling the plug" on her life. We didn't feel that way at all about intubation. We chose that we would intubate because like any other child, our child may get an short term illness like a virus. A regular child who gets a virus might need to get some support from the hospital to make it through. So why wouldn't we give our trisomy child the same chance to get over an acute illness, even if the intervention, intubation, is a little more extreme? We feel more comfortable intubating in the short term to get over a virus and making a decision about life or death after the illness is over, rather than never giving her the support she needs to get over an acute illness. –Lorri

It does not have to be all or nothing. Take each decision as it comes (but educate yourself beforehand), and be open to changing your mind as you follow your child's lead and what is best for them. The absolute best choice we made was not to

terminate, and we will forever be grateful for our two days with Ayven Grace. –Nicole

One of the cardiologists came in....He was so compassionate and spoke with such kindness to us regarding our options for care. He told us heart surgery was still an option if we wanted. One of the most profound things that we took away, and I'm paraphrasing, was, "You're the ones that are going to have to live this life, so make every decision knowing that." And that's really been my anchor in making decisions and advocating all these years. –Paige

Getting on the same page with the medical team

For our first family meeting they wanted to understand what our goals were for our baby, if it was palliative care or full intervention. From there they should adjust their care approach based on their capabilities and also their ethics standpoint. My two cents would be to be very straightforward and clear with what you want for your child... make sure everyone is on the same page. We personally wanted full code and full intervention... it was an uphill battle, but everyone got on board. –Mark

Initially we asked a lot of questions, and the responses we got were along the lines of "We usually do such and such in this kind of situation." Afterward we would talk, and most of the time we didn't like the responses we got. So the next time we went in, instead of asking a question about how they would normally handle it, we said, "This is what we want done; will you do it?" The response we got at that point was, "It's not the way I would do it, but if that is what you want, then yes." As long as they were willing to do what we asked, we didn't see a need to change providers. It required a lot of research on our part, and lots of talking with friends we met along the way, but in the end, we felt like it allowed us to make the best decisions we could and to give our son his best chance at life instead of listening to the doom and gloom from the doctors. –Abbey

It's ok to ask questions. It's ok to help educate the doctor from research you've done. When my little was in the NICU, they were at a loss with certain things. They didn't know who could help, as they hadn't seen a T18 baby in some time. I found a surgeon willing to do her heart repair. My doctor wasn't angry. He was so happy that I was helpful and on it to save her life. He thanked me and asked if he could reach out to me in the future. As blindly as I wanted to go into it, my research and willingness to look things up and ask for help saved her. –Brooke

Different outcomes than expected

It's okay to try new things and take a chance, even in the face of discouragement from medical professionals. I remember Anna's NICU doctors trying to push us to make a decision about a G-tube even though she was doing well with bottle feeding because as a T13 baby she would "never" be able to eat enough to adequately gain weight. Well, they were wrong. At 21 months old, she is completely orally fed and in the 20th percentile for weight! –Megan

The doctors [can be] so negative, especially if you have a prenatal diagnosis, yet they know so little and so much can change. My trisomy 9 mosaic child, Alana, wasn't supposed to walk or talk, and she walks and never, ever stops talking! –Patricia

My daughter was diagnosed via three prenatal echoes to have HLHS [Hypoplastic left heart syndrome], but after birth none of that was detected. Years later, I met a pediatric cardiac

surgeon on my journey and told him of my daughter's changing diagnosis. He wasn't surprised at all, and he said nothing is ever certain until baby is born. So why did nobody ever tell me that prenatally? I think the prenatal providers subconsciously take away all hope because they think it will help those who terminate to heal. –Barb

We were told that Kalee wouldn't have emotions or a personality. That's not true at all. She has the sweetest demeanor, and her emotions are very, very complex. She feels love and understands what love is. She's expressed that she loves me by shaking her head yes and also verbally, even though she's mostly nonverbal. –Robert

Life with a child who has special needs

Every day we have spent with Samuel has been a miracle. A profound blessing that is impossible to put into words. Despite his heart conditions and his severe lung disease, we recognize a will to live on our son's face. We know he wants to be here. He wants to fight. So we keep on following his lead and fighting for his life just as we would do for our other son born without these complications. –Rebekah

I think it's so important for families to know not every baby is the same. You can't compare one child with another. – Jessica

A helpful nurse told me when my son Peter was born with T18, "This is a marathon, not a sprint, so be sure and take care of yourself, too." Another thing that new parents should know is that they can love and parent their child with special needs and help them reach their full potential just like they would their other kids and that these kids are a great blessing. –Mary

Take every setback and struggle as a blessing. Yes, it is hard, but it is a blessing. Mental health matters. It is okay to say you are not okay. It is okay to mourn what you think "normal" should be. Find a good support system if you need one. –Kim

It may sound cliché, but our children are individuals. I had to learn Natalie's rhythm. To her, therapy is one thing at a time, sitting up, or playing with one toy, or singing a song, oral stimulation. All my ideas of what therapy or growth should be—thrown out the window. She has her own pace and learns best in her own way, as much as I want to push and rush her. –Jenny

Find ways to STOP waiting for the other shoe to drop! Enjoy every single moment. Expect nothing and expect everything! (Meaning ...go ahead and have high hopes! And expectations!) These kiddos aren't given enough credit where credit is due. They need a lot of help in the beginning and things might be slow at first, but once you give them a chance, watch out! They will fill your heart with so much love and joy, no matter what. –Melissa

Chapter 12
What Do YOU Say?

Our babies are much stronger than many people give them credit for being, but...some decisions are so hard!
–Ryan

We've looked at ways to research your child's specific diagnosis. We've asked some difficult questions and given space for receiving your medical team's input. And we've taken time to consider what real parents have to say. All of these pieces are incredibly important—but ultimately, what they should all be leading toward is what YOU think is best for YOUR baby. And despite all that you've learned to this point, you may still have questions which seem to have no answers. Medical information, after all, can only take you so far.

Other types of input

If you haven't already done so, you may want to consider reaching out to a spiritual advisor, perhaps a pastor or clergyman if you are already involved in a church and have connections.

While it's true that not all spiritual leaders are necessarily knowledgeable or equipped for this particular situation, many if not most are "in the business," so to speak, of helping people through difficult circumstances. And who knows—perhaps walking with you through your own journey will teach and equip your church leaders to be better prepared for helping someone else in a similar situation in the future!

If you're not ready or comfortable with reaching out to someone in a church setting, perhaps consider working with a counselor or therapist with a background in this type of circumstance who can help you work through the many emotions and potential relationship difficulties that come along with this experience.

Fine-tuning your view of life

You are likely receiving new information on a daily basis and have much to process. As you do so, remember to evaluate everything in light of your foundation. What is truth? Do these new facts and opinions mesh with your foundation? You may find yourself having to fine-tune your view of life.

Value of life. Often medical decisions are framed in what sounds like economic terms. Decision-makers weigh the benefits of preventing a death as well as the implied cost of such actions. Yet to a mother whose growing belly protects a baby with a life-limiting diagnosis, there is no physical way to measure the worth of that precious soul. She longs for the day she can hold her child in her arms, hoping and praying she can meet her baby alive.

In Christian circles there is a concept known as the "sanctity of life." This means that because people are created in God's image, "human life has an inherently sacred attribute that should be protected and respected at all times....The sanctity of life means that humanity is more sacred than the rest of creation."[1] In light of this, a person's value is intrinsic and therefore not dependent on external factors. Those who hold to this view would say we simply cannot assign a quantitative value to a human being.

Quality of life. With the advances in medical technology, quality-of-life issues bring a complexity to ethical decisions that simply didn't exist in ages past. Complicating this issue is the fact that as a mom or dad, these decisions are ultimately up to YOU to make on behalf of your child. It's one thing to create a living will for yourself, deciding ahead of time what medical interventions you do or do not want when you reach the end of your time on earth. But it's quite another task to determine such serious matters for your child, not knowing exactly what he or she may need at birth or beyond. Do you opt for interventions that may potentially get your baby past a precarious phase and allow for the possibility of a longer, stronger life? What if interventions require attachment to machines and you're unable to hold or comfort your baby? If the medical advances ultimately allow your child to live and come home, might it be worth it? But what if the interventions don't work and there is regret for not spending those precious moments snuggling and singing to your baby?

The weight of determining someone else's quality of life (and potentially even length of life) is far heavier than anyone who hasn't gone through this journey can possibly understand. You do not have to go through this alone. Hopefully you have a spouse or partner working through these issues with you. If not (or even if you do), please make sure you find someone who understands this specific journey and is willing to walk through it with you. There are organizations whose sole purpose is to help parents who have chosen to carry a baby with a life-limiting diagnosis to term.[2] It is helpful to reach out to one of these organizations no matter what kind of support system you already have in place, as their resources and connections can provide valuable help during your pregnancy as well as post-delivery.

Overcoming "Analysis Paralysis"

As you make your way toward the next step in this journey—delivering your baby, whatever that will look like—you are taking in so much information. Not only that, but you are also having to filter through more opinions than you may even realize. Sometimes it's hard to separate a medical opinion from fact, or the opinion of a well-meaning loved one from reality.

This is HARD stuff, Mom and Dad! We've discussed this before, but it's so important that I want to reiterate it here:

There are no easy answers, and in fact, there may very well not be any "right" answers.

Perhaps your path will become clear the longer you are on your journey. Perhaps the major decisions will be taken out of your hands, one way or another. Or perhaps you will find yourselves unsure of what to do next, praying desperately for wisdom and clarity. While you are waiting for that illumination, continue to pray, plan, and prepare as best as you can. Nothing is written in stone. Everything can change. Go back to your foundation—get centered on the truth. Trust that whatever happens, you will be guided to make the best decisions for your sweet little one as well as for yourself and your family.

"Mama gut" is a real thing. I believe God gave moms an intuition for all things relevant to their children. Sometimes making a decision based on your instincts is really all you have to go on, and in the absence of any definite data that might otherwise sway you, "Go with your gut."

Parents, give yourself grace. Tons of it. Decisions made from a heart of love will honor your sweet baby. No one but God knows the outcome of this pregnancy. Trust Him with everything, including the precious little life you're carrying.

Ancient words of wisdom

Below I will share some of my favorite passages from Scripture that our family has turned to when we've prayed for wisdom and wrestled with difficult decisions. Perhaps they will be helpful and encouraging for you as well.

Trust in the Lord with all your heart,
and do not lean on your own understanding.
In all your ways acknowledge him,
and he will make straight your paths.
Proverbs 3:5-6

If any of you lacks wisdom, let him ask God, who gives generously to all without reproach, and it will be given him.
James 1:5

Therefore I tell you, do not be anxious about your life, what you will eat or what you will drink, nor about your body, what you will put on. Is not life more than food, and the body more than clothing? Look at the birds of the air: they neither sow nor reap nor gather into barns, and yet your heavenly Father feeds them. Are you not of more value than they? And which of you by being anxious can add a single hour to his span of life? And why are you anxious about clothing? Consider the lilies of the field, how they grow: they neither toil nor spin, yet I tell you, even Solomon in all his glory was not arrayed like one of these. But if God so clothes the grass of the field, which today is alive and tomorrow is thrown into the oven, will he not much more clothe you, O you of little faith? Therefore do not be anxious, saying, "What shall we eat?" or "What shall we drink?" or "What shall we wear?" For the Gentiles seek after all these things, and your heavenly Father knows that you need them all. But seek first the kingdom of God and his righteousness, and all these things will

be added to you. Therefore do not be anxious about tomorrow, for tomorrow will be anxious for itself. Sufficient for the day is its own trouble.
Matthew 6:25-34

Do not be anxious about anything, but in everything by prayer and supplication with thanksgiving let your requests be made known to God. And the peace of God, which surpasses all understanding, will guard your hearts and your minds in Christ Jesus.
Philippians 4:6-7

So teach us to number our days that we may get a heart of wisdom.
Psalm 90:12

SECTION 4

PREPARE YOURSELF

Advocacy

While this journey you are on is scary and uncertain, your child is already here with you. Learning how to enjoy your pregnancy can be very challenging but so rewarding. Equipping yourself with the knowledge needed to advocate for yourself and your child will help you have a more positive experience.

–Rhonda Yarrington, co-founder of The Bella Grace Foundation

Because we advocated and pursued full interventions, our Addilyn is five. Because we advocated and pursued interventions, I know of at least a dozen children with [the same diagnosis] who have received care at our state's Children's Hospital that they wouldn't have been able to receive otherwise. Because we advocated time and time again, our girl is here and living life to the fullest.

–Paige

Chapter 13

Enjoying Your Pregnancy

It's ok for families to be excited about the possibilities. It's ok to have baby showers and plan birthday parties. There is so much that's scary with this journey. Always embrace the joy when you can. That's what gets you through when things are hard.

–Kayse

The previous section of this book, with its focus on educating yourself and growing in awareness of what your baby needs and what you and your family may face in the future, has an unavoidable heaviness as you take so much information into consideration and ponder the difficult decisions to come. Likewise, in this next section, as we speak to the advocacy portion of your journey, we must touch on yet more challenging issues. But let's not forget that at the center of all this is a beautiful, precious LIFE. It is so easy to lose sight of the simple joys that are part of this experience—joys that exist in spite of that diagnosis hanging over your head. And so I must advocate for YOU, sweet mama! I desire for you to make the most of each day! I regret spending so much of my pregnancy with Verity feeling anxious and overwhelmed. While those feelings are understandable, of course, my hope and prayer for you is that you can minimize those negative emotions and maximize the time you have with your baby.

Your baby is very much a part of your family pre-birth! Those precious movements, ultrasounds, and heartbeats are extra meaningful during a pregnancy journey like this. Don't wait for the "what ifs" to start making memories with your sweet baby. If you've never done a maternity photo shoot before, now is a great time to schedule one. As one of the moms in our support group said, "I'm getting family photos done so that I can have a family photo with my baby alive." Her baby had an extremely rare condition (triploidy), and while her medical team was supportive of providing needed interventions, this sweet baby girl did not survive the difficult labor and delivery. Those family photos are extra precious, as they record a time when Mama still felt her little girl safe inside her womb.

Here are some other ideas for being intentional during your pregnancy to make memories and cherish the time you have with your baby. Though these circumstances bring about so many strong emotions, it is so precious and important to find joy and meaning in your journey, cherishing ***now*** instead of worrying about ***then***.

Ideas for making memories during the pregnancy

Photos. Take lots of pictures! Especially if you have other children, take photos of your belly with the older sibling(s). You can create a special album with the photos and some of your journaled thoughts. Maybe even make this a family effort, with everyone writing their memories of the experience to include with the photos. What memories do you WANT to make with your child(ren)? What places do you want to see? What experiences do you want to have? Don't wait to tackle some items on that "Bucket List!" Make the most of even the seemingly mundane experiences. "Baby's trip to the ice cream shop" is a wonderful memory to make as Mama gets to pick her favorite flavor!

Movements. Some parents opt for additional ultrasounds, such as a 4D scan during which you can get a recording of Baby's movements. Informal videos of Mom's belly moving while Baby does internal gymnastics are also fun, although sometimes hard to capture! Have fun as a family creating your own videos to commemorate the movements of the life inside.

Special sounds. Record Baby's heartbeat. You can even put a copy of the heartbeat recording inside a stuffed animal, an especially precious way for an older sibling to feel connected. Record your other children talking to their baby brother or sister, maybe reading stories or singing songs.

Intentional and thoughtful activities. Combine self-care with Baby care. Soak in a soothing hot bath and watch your belly dance. Go for a walk with Baby and describe what you're seeing. Or sit in a favorite chair with a favorite drink, close your eyes, and feel those little hands and feet jabbing at your rib cage. Imagine what your baby looks like and pray for your sweet little one. Read favorite books, poems, and Bible stories and verses to Baby. Both Mom and Dad can do this—it can be a good way to connect with your spouse also on this difficult journey.

Written thoughts. Write letters to your baby. There is a special section for this in the *From Diagnosis to Delivery* pregnancy journal we've written. In case you don't already have a copy of that, here are some prompts to get your creative juices flowing:

- How Mommy and Daddy met
- How you felt when you learned you were pregnant
- What it's like to feel Baby moving and how Daddy feels when he sees or feels your belly moving

- Who are the special people who already love Baby?
- What are your hopes, dreams, fears for Baby?
- Who might Baby look like? What color hair, eyes?
- Special quotes
- Bible verses
- Inspirational thoughts of hope and courage
- Stories of other children living with the same diagnosis
- How do you picture celebrating the birth? The one-month birthday? The one-year mark?
- Write about Baby's siblings and what their thoughts are about having a little brother or sister.
- Are there promises you'd like to make to Baby?

What other ideas do you have for making memories during your pregnancy?

What I'd want others to know is enjoy the moments, the swollen feet (no matter how bad they are), the sharp jabs, the baby hiccups, everything, because those are moments we aren't getting back. Time is precious, and each kick is a reminder that our baby is alive and living their best life in our belly.

–Staci

Chapter 14
What About a Baby Shower?

Enjoy the pregnancy. Announce it early on and let others in on your journey. Ask them to pray with you. Join the support groups and start learning. Have the baby shower and buy the baby items. This precious life is worth all of it!
–Candace

The idea of planning a shower for a baby who may or may not live can cause consternation. Personally, I believe every single life is worth celebrating! While your particular needs probably look quite different than those of a "typical" pregnancy, the fact is, you and your sweet babe deserve the opportunity to be showered with blessings.

I hope you have someone in your life with whom you can bring up this sensitive topic. Even better, maybe a close friend or family member has already approached you to ask what you would like to do concerning a baby shower. If not, let's assume the best—the people who love you have probably thought about this but really are not sure how to bring it up or what might be appropriate given the circumstances. If you like the idea of having a special event honoring the life of your precious baby, but no one has brought up the conversation with you, let me gently encourage YOU to speak up. This is good practice for advocating for yourself and your baby! Others around you will follow your lead. Sure, we wish other people would take the initiative. We wish they would intuitively know what we need, what would be meaningful to us, what would help us feel loved and cared for. But the truth is, people do NOT know unless we tell them. Even the kindest, most empathetic friend simply will not understand what this journey is like (unless, of course, she has also experienced something similar). And it could very well be that your friends and family members are so concerned about your feelings that they're afraid even mentioning the idea of a baby shower might cause you pain.

So first, decide if this is indeed something you would like to do (or have done on your behalf). If so, this chapter will be helpful for you and anyone who will help coordinate your special event.

Before or after birth?

As you consider your situation, decide which of the following scenarios seems to be the best fit: a celebration of life while you are still pregnant, or a shower after Baby is born, when you have a better idea of what you will need.

How do you choose? One practical factor may be whether or not this is your first child. Do you already have baby items you can use, such as a car seat, crib, etc.? If not, you may decide to have a more traditional shower. As difficult as it is to consider, items that end up being unused can either be returned or else saved for your future children. Many mothers of babies who have passed away found joy and comfort in being able to use baby clothes and equipment for their "rainbow babies." (A child born after a miscarriage, stillbirth, or infant loss is often called a rainbow baby.) Others take comfort in donating these types of items to other families or a pregnancy resource center.

A practical solution

One option no matter when your special event is held is for your loved ones to bless you with money or gift cards. Our church planned a money tree shower three weeks before our due date. Since we had no idea what lay ahead of us—and since we had 8 other children—this seemed a practical yet thoughtful and generous idea. We received cash as well as gift cards (Visa, Amazon, and restaurant), all of which were helpful as we navigated being separated during the days our daughter was in the NICU. This also gave us time to determine exactly what our needs were.

Gift ideas

If this is your first baby, or if your other children are older and you don't have baby items on hand, you may opt for the more traditional shower. Gift ideas may include:

- Crib/bassinet/pack-and-play
- Stroller
- Car seat
- Changing table
- Preemie clothes
- Bows and hats
- Diapers and wipes (these are usually provided while in the hospital)
- Nursing pillow (for holding Baby even if he/she isn't able to nurse)
- Outfits with buttons instead of zippers to fit cords for monitors and tubes

- Socks and onesies
- Tummy time mat
- Breast pump if desiring to nurse and/or provide breast milk through a feeding tube

Other ideas to commemorate your special situation:
- Personalized blanket (wonderful for photos)
- Hand and foot molding kits
- Memorial garden stone
- Memorial picture frames
- Memory box
- Stuffed animal with recording device—you can record baby's heartbeat.
- Molly Bear (see mollybears.org)
- Walter Bear (see waltersbears.com)
- Special jewelry, such as:
    - Locket for holding a photo or other memento
    - Bracelet or necklace with Baby's name on it
    - Birthstone jewelry

Meal delivery

A meal train is a thoughtful provision, no matter what happens with the delivery. At our church shower, people brought frozen meals in disposable containers, so we had our freezer stocked and prepared before I went into labor. With online scheduling options, coordinating meal delivery can be set up ahead of time. Food allergies and sensitivities (as well as food aversions) can be noted along with other practical instructions for communication and delivery. Schedule meals to be brought every other day or maybe three times a week. This may depend on your family size, of course, but often the problem becomes too many leftovers! And keep in mind that Mom and/or Dad may be spending time at the hospital, where meal vouchers are often provided.

Meals are also appreciated in the event that Baby passes. The last thing any mama wants to do is figure out what to feed everyone, especially if she has no appetite and is consumed with grief.

Moms, advocate for yourself and your family ahead of time if at all possible—ask someone to be in charge of a meal train at the appropriate time. If you can communicate the necessary details early on, your helper can take charge and have everything in place when the time comes, leaving you with one less thing to be concerned about when you are fully occupied with more important matters.

If I were talking to my past self, I would tell myself to allow people to buy things ready for her arrival. I stopped my family spending money on her, or purchasing stuff in case she didn't make it out alive. I realize now that was taking some of their joy away, and it meant I only had secondhand items for her. I'd tell myself that having hope dashed is no less painful than not having hope at all. She'll be 10 in August!

–Caroline

Chapter 15

Preparing for Loss

It's difficult to prepare mentally, because no one truly knows how well a baby may or may not do until the birth. Much may be known, but much more is unknown.

–Sarah

No one can ever truly prepare for the gravity of child loss. Yet one thing I hear from parents who endure this agony is that while they knew this was a possibility given their child's diagnosis, they didn't really think it would happen to them. When the baby was stillborn, or when the child passed shortly after birth, parents often felt completely unprepared. This may seem somewhat surprising, given how much time we spend during the pregnancy considering the possibility of losing our baby, and yet when reality hits, it is often nothing like what we had imagined.

Dawn's experience with Athena (see chapter 9) brought her to a new level of knowledge and awareness. Dawn is an example of a mother who threw her heart and soul into researching about her child's condition, reaching out to various organizations to find up-to-date information to take to her medical team. Though she received some pushback initially about supporting her daughter at birth (because of the prenatal diagnosis), eventually the team got on board, and because of Dawn's advocating efforts, everyone was prepared to give Athena whatever life-saving interventions she would need upon delivery. Unfortunately, the situation was far more critical than anyone had anticipated, and Athena lived just one day on earth.

As Dawn shared with me later, part of her grieving stemmed from feeling that she wasn't given the full picture up front—she felt that learning about medical interventions and interacting with parents whose children were thriving helped to set Athena on a similar path. She writes, "I was not prepared for losing her at all. I think we need as a whole community to prepare women more for this. I was so focused on the interventions, it distracted me from making the most of every second I had with Athy as I was in denial, thinking, 'Something can always be done.' But sometimes, things cannot be done! Nothing can be done!"

Dawn was one of the early members of our From Diagnosis to Delivery support group, so involved with our community. Even now she continues to reach out to other parents, blessing and encouraging them from her vantage point of being farther along the path of loving a child with a life-limiting condition.

It is in honor of Dawn, her husband, and their sweet Athena that I sit down to write this chapter. They represent so many other families whose world came crashing down around them the day their child left behind an earthly body. As Dawn observed, "Sometimes, no matter how hard we advocate, no matter what interventions, it won't change the outcome—and that issue somehow needs to be communicated, too."

Thus we continue this section of the book focusing on advocacy with a difficult yet necessary look at what it means to prepare for loss. Perhaps it seems like a contradiction to think of being an advocate at the same time you consider being a bereaved parent. While it is true that we mostly identify the advocacy role in the medical setting, let's broaden the definition to apply to anything relevant to your precious child—which includes his or her precious parents as well as the legacy you create as a family.

Consider, then: what is important to YOU when you think about the experience you will have when it's time to meet your baby face to face? We aren't talking about a birth plan yet—we will consider that later. This is much more intimate and personal than the mechanics of labor and delivery. While we absolutely desire for you to feel prepared to advocate for the appropriate physical care your baby may need, right now we will focus on the mental, emotional, and spiritual aspects of caring for your child—meaning what that looks like for you as the mother and father.

With that in mind, what are the important, meaningful activities you would wish to experience with your baby? Are there special rituals you have always imagined doing at child birth? Special things you did with your other babies (if you have other children)? In the event your baby is stillborn or passes soon after birth, are there things you would regret NOT doing?

The regret factor is what we hope to avoid (or at least minimize) as we consider these difficult questions. If you experience pre-term labor, or if things don't progress the way you expect and hope at the time of delivery, things may be happening at such a whirlwind pace all around you that you can hardly be expected to make on-the-spot decisions. As much as possible, think through some of these questions and ideas ahead of time so you can have a meaningful experience despite the trauma and grief. Even if you don't endure the loss of your child immediately, it is more likely than not that you will one day face the time when your child succumbs to the complications of that life-limiting diagnosis. While decisions at that point may not necessarily need to be made in such a rush, it might be helpful to come back to some of the ideas and suggestions in this chapter.

As you look at some of the memory-making ideas shared by other moms who have gone through this journey, think about preparing a special bag with the items you would want or need in order to actually do these activities at the hospital—for example, items to get fingerprints, footprints, and molds. This can then be kept with your hospital bag to have ready as the moment demands.

Preparing your other children

If you have other children, it is important to be open and honest with them about what is going on. While this is a difficult topic, it is my personal opinion and experience that children will do better when they are given bits of information at multiple times throughout this journey. Use appropriate language to help them understand the situation.[1] You don't have to sugar coat the diagnosis, nor do you need to hide the seriousness of the matter. Children take their cues from the adults in their lives, and while they may not understand everything, they will find comfort and security in hearing directly from Mommy and Daddy about the strange things happening around them.

Conversations with older children might be difficult as they ask questions to which you don't yet have answers. As a family, this is the time to be open and honest with your thoughts and feelings, deepening connections while allowing everyone the space needed to process the situation.

I didn't have much opportunity to plan out what to say to our other kids—they were all in the kitchen and heard my side of the conversation when we got the phone call from the doctor. They could tell I was emotional, and I couldn't simply brush off that devastating news. So we were pretty frank about everything from the very beginning. I did sit down in the following weeks and wrote some text specifically directed toward our younger children to explain to them how their baby sister would be different. I wanted to be thoughtful and intentional about how to prepare them for the physical differences they would see in Baby Verity as well as the possibility that she might not come home from the hospital. An artist friend illustrated the text, and in the end we created a children's book that has also been helpful for other families on this journey.[2]

However you choose to explain the diagnosis and its potential ramifications, engage in ongoing dialogue with your children. Sarah, mother of Hannah, who lived 13 days, says, "I wish we had talked with [our other children] more about the possibility that our baby might die. We prepared them about having a sibling with Down syndrome and learned with them about her heart defect, but we did not prepare them much for the possibility that she might not come home. That preparation happened later out of necessity, but it was a lot for them to process in a shorter amount of time."

A mantra that some families adopt on this journey is "Prepare for the worst, hope for the best." This might be a good guiding principle for you as you talk with your other children (and extended family members, for that matter) about whatever their expectations are concerning your baby. Consider a "what if" dialogue with your children as a way to probe their thoughts and gauge their understanding. "What if you get to meet Baby in the hospital? What would you like to say to her? What if Baby goes to heaven when she's still little?"

As you think about what your own desires are when it comes to meeting your baby in person, consider involving your other children in the idea-generating process, obviously taking into account their ages and level of understanding. While their ideas and whims may change from day to day, see if there is something they can latch onto that will hold significance and meaning for them when they look back on this experience. Maybe a favorite book or stuffed animal, or perhaps matching shirts or hats, can be incorporated into routines done during the pregnancy and then carried into the delivery room for photos and video to capture.

Ideas for making memories after delivery

These are all meaningful things to do no matter what happens with your baby! Love and cherish your sweet little one in life and in loss.

- Sing to Baby. Sing the songs that are special to you and your family, whether hymns, nursery rhymes, Christmas carols, or silly children's songs. Or perhaps have a play list ready so your favorite music can play softly in the background.
- Talk to Baby. Let him hear your voice. Tell him about his family and all who love him. Pray with and for him. Read special stories or Scriptures.
- Hold Baby close. Have skin-to-skin time with her so you can feel her soft little body, kiss her little head, study her unique features.
- If at all possible, get professional photographs. If you don't know someone personally who is willing to do this for you, reach out to the organization Now I Lay Me Down to Sleep. They provide photographers for just such occasions. Perhaps consider the types of photos you would like: close-ups of hands, feet, face, ears; your wedding rings on toes/feet; Baby's and parents' hands; Baby with each family member; Baby with any special gifts, stuffed animals, blankets, outfits.
- Along with photos, videos are cherished memories as well. One mom said she videoed herself singing special songs to her baby just for herself to watch later.

- Bathe and dress Baby. Comb and brush hair, maybe cutting a lock of hair to save. Use a favorite lotion or essential oils so in the future the same aroma will bring back these special memories.
- Have your pastor/clergy visit—some families desire Baby to be baptized or receive a special blessing at the hospital. Get photos and videos of these special moments.
- Arrange for other special people in your life to visit the hospital. Make a plan for notifying these people when you go into labor so you aren't trying to remember whom to contact in between contractions! Make sure you get photos and videos as desired.
- Journal each day. If you are in the NICU for an extended time, consider our *Navigating the NICU* journal[3] for an easy way to record Baby's stats, important medical observations, a note of gratitude, and your own thoughts and emotions.
- Some families have special items made (such as t-shirts, hats, bracelets, etc.) so that long-distance family and friends can feel like part of the experience and show support. (Sometimes this can be done as a fundraiser as well if funds are needed for expenses.) Photos of people wearing those items can bring the feelings of support and connection closer to home.
- Many keepsakes can be made from hand, feet, and finger prints as well as hand and foot molds. Jewelry and framed art pieces are just a couple of examples. One family put their son's footprint in their favorite book.
- Breast milk jewelry is also a keepsake option. Some mothers choose to pump breast milk for a time and donate the milk when their child passes; others find this too painful emotionally. Either way, Mama, consider how you will care for your body in this way, as your body will not know whether or not you are bringing home your baby. The natural course of milk production can be painful physically as well as

mentally and emotionally when there is loss. Speak with a lactation consultant or anyone on your medical team about how to handle this. (Cabbage leaves are helpful…)

Cuddle Cots

A Cuddle Cot is a special system to slow down the natural process that follows death. This allows the baby to remain with the family, allowing for more time to process what is happening and make special memories. The benefits are recognized across the world: Cuddle Cots are used extensively in the United Kingdom, across Europe, in Australia, and are becoming more popular in the United States as well. The cooling pad can be used in any bassinet, crib, or bed. This may be a good option for the family to give them precious hours to bond, have photos and plaster molds taken, and allow extended family to meet the baby. You can ask your medical team if this is an option they provide at the hospital where you deliver. If not, there are multiple non-profit organizations that help families access Cuddle Cots. If this is something you might wish to utilize, perhaps someone close to you can help you research your options.

The logistics of loss

Cremation? Casket? Funeral? Celebration of life service?

These are not decisions any parent should have to make, but sadly it is a reality for many whose children have life-limiting diagnoses. While we can't be sure that these children will NOT make it to term, it is helpful to have at least considered what might or must happen if your baby passes away. One of the hardest conversations my husband and I had after receiving Verity's diagnosis was the day he came home from work and told me he had learned we could bury our daughter at the Air Force Academy cemetery, which is where my husband intends to be buried when his time comes. At the time we lived in Iowa; the Academy is located in Colorado. I cried at the thought of transporting our little girl across state lines, but when we considered the options, we felt this would be our plan. While we have not yet, at the time of this writing, experienced the loss of our daughter—the plan is in place for the day when we have to say goodbye.

When making these decisions, expenses are often a burden on families. Be assured that there are options available to help financially. Some funeral homes, for example, will offer free services for infants, but be sure to ask about age restrictions—is a four-month-old considered an infant? Some free services are only given in the event Baby passes at 14 days old or sooner, others may go up to six months or a year. Various charities and foundations can provide financial coverage for certain expenses, so don't be afraid to reach out and ask for help.

This is another area in which a trusted family member or close friend can be of assistance. Whom do you know who might be able and willing to take on the role of funeral planner? Allowing someone else to help shoulder this burden will ease your already overloaded mind and reduce your stress level. Even with a helper, you'll need to determine ahead of time what you and your spouse or partner will find meaningful in these circumstances.

Planning a service

Sarah shares, "Looking back, I am so glad we had a memorial service for Hannah. This was important for our family, especially for extended family who did not get to meet Hannah in person. It brought closure."

Will you want a viewing? A funeral service? A graveside ceremony? Some families call their gathering a "Celebration of Life" service. I've also attended services long-distance via livestream and written in online "guest books" to offer support and share how these precious children touched me even so far away. Some parents ask attendees to wear bright colors, or maybe a particular color to represent awareness of their child's diagnosis. They may choose to plan for a time of music, food, and fellowship after a more somber time of reflection. This event can and should be what YOU want it to be. This is a time to honor the life of your precious little one. It is no less significant just because it was all too brief—in fact, you may find your journey has had a powerful effect on your community in large part ***because*** of its brevity.

If you are members of a church, start by asking your pastor and leadership staff about the type of event you are planning. Some churches have committees to help families who are in this situation. They can walk you through the planning process and tell you what kinds of help they typically provide as well as connect you with other local resources. If you aren't already connected to a church, perhaps reach out to those you know who are. Often you can use a church property for a memorial service with either zero or minimal costs. If you would like to have time for people to eat and fellowship after the service, be sure to ask about whether the location can accommodate this.

Given the nature of this journey, you may have strong feelings about how many people you feel you can handle at a memorial service. Some parents are naturally more reserved and choose not to share the details of diagnosis and delivery with very many outside their closest circles. If this is you, do not feel pressured into having a large funeral service! It is completely acceptable to have a small, private viewing (if desired) and service/burial. However, if you have been sharing with a larger circle of people for awhile, perhaps even publicly blogging or posting about your journey, you may feel comfortable with a bigger event that could accommodate more people. Just give yourself lots of space during and after the event—we may feel strong enough to "get through" something only to be overwhelmed in the moment.

Both parents and even siblings should have input into what the memorial service should involve. Consider what songs or musical selections would be meaningful. Do you have musical family members or friends who would appreciate being involved in this way and could handle the potential stress of a performance during a sensitive occasion? Are there special people you would like to speak or pray at the event? Would you yourself like to share anything? Perhaps you would like to write something out for someone else to read if you don't think you'd be up to speaking in public (perfectly understandable). If you have other children, maybe they would like to write something out to be shared, or maybe they would like to read something they've written out beforehand. What would you like people to know and remember about your child? About your journey personally, as a couple, as a family? A bereaved family can bless and encourage their community by sharing testimonies of faith under fire. Your thoughts and stories about this journey can be shared verbally from a platform or in written form, perhaps in a program or as part of a video shared during the service.

Think about the photos and video clips you'd like others to enjoy. There are many talented folks who would be glad to help you assemble a special video compilation to show at the service—or perhaps this is something you enjoy doing and would find therapeutic if you were to do it yourself. Additionally, you may wish to choose special items to represent your child or that hold special significance for you. You or someone else can arrange these items on a display table, perhaps along with a guest book for people to sign.

Cremation or casket?

If you haven't already had a conversation with your spouse or partner about cremation vs. a casket, start that difficult discussion sooner rather than later.

Some families choose cremation. Though a difficult task, some parents appreciate the opportunity to seek out a special urn so they can keep their babies "at home" with everyone else in the family. There are many beautiful options available that can provide a fitting visual tribute to your baby whenever you see the urn, which can be part of a special shelf, mantle, or wall space where you display other meaningful keepsakes. Families who choose this option feel it is a way to keep their babies closer to their hearts rather than separating themselves physically.

Other families prefer a more traditional setting, laying their child to rest in a tiny casket buried in the local cemetery. (This is not the only option: I know one family whose 5-month-old son rests in his own little grave in their backyard.) Parents can then make time to visit their baby's grave, appreciating peaceful, quiet moments of reflection. They bring siblings; they bring flowers; they bring picnics. Honoring their little one at a removed location allows them to be intentional with their "time together" and then (somehow) move back into "normal life." (Nothing is ever normal again, though. This we know.)

One concern some families have expressed is determining the location for laying their little one to rest. If there isn't already a purchased family plot, you can look into a temporary mausoleum in your city until permanent arrangements can be made.

Words of wisdom from parents whose children have passed.

When Hannah was born, I was so scared to hold her. I just couldn't face my dead daughter. But after the nurse handed her to me, she was so beautiful. I held her for two days. Even though she had gone to heaven, I needed that time to bond with her, to feel a connection. It was the hardest, most beautiful thing I've ever done. Even now, I can feel her weight on my chest. I can smell her soft hair and feel the smoothness of her skin. I would encourage anyone that was in my situation to use the time you have with your child to make memories, form a bond and be close to their body. It was just such a special time. –Sarah

After [our son] passed, they did some heart tests on me, and my hubby took him to a private room, played worship music, and walked around with him. When he came back, we took photos of him. His hands and feet and us together, his perfect cheeks from every angle. His hair which was exactly like his dad's as a teenager.... I think there can never be enough videos or photos of our sweet little miracles who forever change us. [The hospice place] took his hand prints and feet prints, and we loved those so much. Pendants were made for all three of us. They are my favorite keepsake. –Kitrina

Charis was one of my greatest joys and gifts in life. I would take a hundred of her. As scary as the diagnosis and unknowns sound, and as challenging as daily life can be with a medically complex child, and as hard as it's been since losing her, I would do it over and over again. What a privilege and blessing it was to carry her, to bring her into this world, and to spend seventeen precious months with her. She was beautiful and miraculous and an absolute gift from God! –Candace

For 9 months, my life was walking on eggshells it seemed. I finally gave birth to my sweet girl. My only goal was to be able to hold her and feel her warm body against mine. And I did. For 9 months, my job was to give her a safe environment and when she came earth side, I wanted her to take lead on what she needed. And we did just that. Just shortly after birth we were given challenges after challenges. She showed us what she needed from us. After 8 days we knew she needed to go back home...And on June 18th, I held her one last time and tucked her in one last time as she took her last breath on my chest. It was the hardest thing I've ever had to do. –Flower Evangeline

My advice to anyone going through this is don't be afraid of them passing away. It can be beautiful. When Miles passed away, it was calm and peaceful. He was on my chest and stayed there until we were ready. His siblings held him and kissed him. The nurses took fingerprints and made a necklace. And anything that touched him they saved for us. We had T-shirts made for friends and family who couldn't be there as a way to support us, and it really helped when we were feeling down and alone. I love seeing them wearing the shirts even after he passed. I cherish every moment we had with Miles and tried really hard to document as much of his life as possible. –Lauren

My son who should have passed away immediately gave us the most precious gift. An amazing 32 hours. I had the honor of singing our song to him in person. Of holding him. Of studying every detail of his cute little body and overlapped fingers. It's funny how the first marker of clenched hands that made me sick to the stomach in the beginning was the very thing I loved the most about him in person. The differences and defects that bring such fear while within the womb just seem to dissipate when you're in person. You see them as your perfect little baby. A being you didn't know you could love so immensely. –Jennifer

Rhett came early, despite so many efforts to stop labor. We met face to face on April 9th, and I got over 5 beautiful, glorious hours with him earth side where he was loved on the entire time and didn't know pain. I'm going to tell you all, this journey is not easy. None of it is. But no matter the outcome, it's all worth it. All of it. I'd do it again to have that time with my boy again. He was the most beautifully perfect baby I've ever seen. I praise God today, instead of letting the grief sweep me away, that I got to be Rhett's mama. That I got to know his precious face and rub my cheeks on all his hair. Please know that that love will get you through—all of it. And that these babies have a purpose, no matter how long we have them. My life is forever changed for the better because of my little Rhett, and his story isn't over yet. –Jen

Hannah came over a month early. We knew she had trisomy 21 and a serious heart defect but were surprised by an early Caesarean arrival due to blood clots and stroke that damaged her brain. When we were facing the likelihood of her death, I realized that though I knew with my head that she might die, I didn't really believe that she would. It was good to remain hopeful, but eventually I had to accept "the way things actually were," and continually adjust my expectations to match reality. –Sarah

Losing a child is an indescribable experience. For myself no amount of imagining what it might be like or feel like even came close to the pain I truly feel since losing BellaGrace. I cling tightly to my faith that I will be reunited with her again in Heaven, and that is the only thing that keeps me going. –Rhonda

Chapter 16

Preparing for Life

One thing I learned very quickly is that while the NICU and PICU staff were very competent and caring, they knew little about [my daughter's specific diagnosis]. In some circumstances, this went beyond traditional advocacy. We had to teach the medical community about trisomy 18 and specifically [about our daughter] Charis. This can feel rather intimidating at times, especially if you disagree with the doctor or team at any given time. Prepare yourself for the task. It's important and necessary to find your voice and not be afraid to use it.

–Candace

Preparing for your baby to live despite a life-limiting diagnosis includes researching, planning, and communicating on a whole new level. Before we dive into some specifics, let me assure you that there are people whose entire job it is to help parents like you navigate these paths. I was so afraid of not knowing what to do or whom to call for help, but someone met us at every point in our journey and walked us through whatever our next step was at that time. Of course, I firmly believe God ultimately ordered our steps and sent amazing human beings to help us! Looking back, I am so grateful things seemed to fall into place, because we did not have a clue what we needed. We may not have felt adequately prepared, but as it turns out, we had what we needed when we needed it. Hopefully this chapter will give you better preparation than we had so you can be more proactive and not have to depend on chance!

Fair care

Because of the severity of Addilyn's heart defects, we knew full interventions was the only way she would have a chance at all. We had to be very involved in all aspects of her care and ask questions about everything. We've met some brilliant and caring doctors and medical professionals, but we have also met some that don't agree with Addilyn receiving full interventions, so their care is really lacking. –Paige

As you consider what interventions you wish to be provided for your baby, please be sure you are having honest, open conversations with your medical team. There are too many examples of babies who have a life-limiting diagnosis being denied access to the same care and interventions that other children would automatically receive. While we do not wish by any means to insinuate that all hospitals are hostile toward or even dismissive of these precious lives, we do urge parents to be aware, ask for additional opinions, and understand there is a possibility of facing discrimination when seeking the best care possible for your little one. If you feel your child is being denied certain life-saving measures simply because of the diagnosis, it is your right to request second and third opinions and to transfer your baby to the care of physicians who are supportive and prepared to provide those interventions.

Insurance and financial considerations

Just general high risk pregnancy info that I've learned: call your insurance company and make sure you have a really solid understanding of your coverage! You most likely will be referred to a number of different providers, so make sure you understand your coverage and call your insurance when you get a new referral to find out if that new provider is covered, etc. In a perfect world your doctor would only refer you to people that your insurance covers, but that's not always the case! You may need to ask your insurance for authorization to see a provider that's "out of network" if they are the only option willing to provide you care! –Emma

You should be able to access a case manager through your primary/private insurance who can help you with your questions. Get as much information ahead of time as you can. Share what you know about your child's diagnosis and potential needs to find out what kinds of interventions, surgeries, medical devices and equipment, and so on will be covered as well as what you need to do when the time comes. Having a contact for communication is invaluable, as you will most likely be navigating mountains of paperwork, evaluations, and appointments.

Depending on your child's diagnosis, he or she may be eligible to receive coverage through Medicaid. One option is based on the parents' income, so if you are within the income guidelines, then this would be offered regardless of diagnosis. Another option is to access Medicaid through a waiver program, which is helpful for families who might otherwise be disqualified from receiving aid due to income that exceeds the threshold. The Medicaid waiver option is not based on your financial situation at all—only your child's medical condition—and therefore the benefits are ONLY for the child with medical needs (not the whole family). Medicaid, then, would not replace your primary insurance, but it would be the secondary insurance option for that child.

Each state has its own process to navigate, but there should be a waiver available for those with a medically complex condition. Please know that a diagnosis is not a guarantee; some states have more stringent requirements than others. You will need to collect as much information as possible to show the needs of your child—for example, letters and notes from doctors and therapists. The process of applying does take a few months, possibly longer. Some plans will allow backdating to the child's birth date or the date you started the process. Even if you are still pregnant, it's all right to be proactive to get this process started.

You will want to connect with someone who can help you with the paperwork. We did this through our early intervention services starting when Verity was about six months old. Through The Resource Exchange, we met with several different people over the course of the application process. Job titles will vary depending on the program; our contacts are "Navigation Coordinators." These people are experts in working through certain portions of the process, and we were "handed off" from one person to the next as we jumped through the various hoops. When all was said and done, we were given a Medicaid card and have since been able to list it as a supplemental insurance option for Verity. There have been times when Medicaid helped us pay for adaptive equipment not covered by our primary insurance. Additionally, Medicaid helps us cover home health care as well so that we do not pay out of pocket for home nursing.

Regardless of your insurance situation, tuck away funds for emergencies and medical care that isn't covered. If you don't yet have an emergency and/or medical fund set up, please consider including this in your monthly budget so you can grow a cushion to help when the unexpected happens.

Early intervention services

"Early Intervention" is the term used to describe services and support available for babies and young children, from birth through 36 months, who have developmental delays and disabilities. This usually encompasses services such as speech, occupational, and physical therapies, depending on the particular needs of the child. These services are publicly funded, provided to those in need because of how significantly they can affect children and help them overcome challenges that come with a particular diagnosis or disability. Typically the services are provided free of charge or at a reduced rate.

At birth or soon after, your family should be connected with someone either at the hospital or someone associated with these services if it seems appropriate. If you are unsure, just ask! You can always call your state's early intervention program directly and ask for your child to be evaluated to see if he or she is eligible for services.

We were given information about the Iowa early intervention services before we left the NICU. The brochure went into the stack of paperwork we were collecting during our time at the hospital, and who knows when I would have found the time, energy, and courage to make a phone call. Thankfully, the information went both ways, and someone from the Iowa services reached out to us first. We scheduled an evaluation and were receiving services before Verity was two months old.

When the military sent us to our next assignment a couple of months later, the Iowa folks proactively connected us with the Colorado team, who reached out to us before we unpacked. An evaluation meeting was scheduled, and we began meeting with our occupational and physical therapists weekly thereafter. Speech therapy was added to our care plan after Verity received her BAHA (bone-assisted hearing aid). Verity received attentive care from our therapists, who came to our home and worked around our schedule. We remain friends with these ladies today, and in fact our physical therapist continues to provide in-home therapy for Verity through our private insurance now that Verity has "aged out" of early intervention, which ends on a child's third birthday. (The fact that we have surpassed that milestone brings me to tears—God is still writing our girl's story here on earth!)

Specialty care providers

A medically complex child will usually have a team of specialists instead of seeing only one pediatrician. The early months of Verity's life were incredibly full, as she had a variety of tests, evaluations, and surgeries. We did not necessarily know ahead of time all that the early months would entail, although we did expect she would likely need some help with feeding based on the fact that many other children with a trisomy diagnosis had some kind of feeding tube. Had I known what was coming, would I have been better prepared? Or would I have been even more overwhelmed than I already was?! There's no way to know, but perhaps having a bit of a heads-up can help YOU mentally prepare for the early days and weeks with your special sweetie if by God's grace you are able to take your baby home.

Hopefully you will receive a work-up at the hospital after delivery so that you will have some ideas of what your baby will need as far as assessments and specialty care in the days following discharge. You may already know, for example, that because of a heart condition you will need to consult with a cardiology team. Other things may come as a surprise. Hold your plans loosely and be prepared to fill your calendar with a number of appointments. Be sure you are communicating with your insurance provider(s) as well.

This is also time to be checking in with your support groups and connections with others who are caring for children with the same diagnosis as your baby. Don't be afraid to ask for input regarding what types of evaluations and specialty appointments you should be asking about. For example, I would not have known to ask for a swallow study if I hadn't heard from my network that Trisomy 18 children are in danger of silently aspirating.

In the first year of her life, Verity had the following tests: multiple echocardiograms, brain scan, upper GI series, swallow study, pH probe, renal scans, sleep study, VCUG (voiding cystourethrogram to check bladder draining), barium enema (to examine the colon), and sedated ABR (hearing test). We met with specialists from the following areas: genetics, cardiology, urology, audiology, orthopedics, gastroenterology, pulmonology, and otolaryngology (ENT). And she received occupational, physical, and speech therapy at home. This was a LOT to deal with, as you can imagine! (And we had eight other children still living at home with us!) While Verity is still followed by a number of specialty doctors, our schedule is not nearly as hectic as that first year.

Your little one may or may not have so many tests and appointments—but be aware that if your child overcomes the odds and comes home with you, there likely will be more visits to the doctor and/or hospital than with a newborn who does not have the same life-limiting diagnosis.

Home health care

Depending on your child's needs and the resources provided by your state and community, you may qualify to receive home health care services. I did not think this would be an option for our family, as I thought my military officer husband's income would be above the threshold for services such as this. However, just as the Medicaid waiver was available for Verity based solely on her needs, we learned we could also receive home nursing services (if we desired) based on her condition.

If you ask any group of special needs parents what they think of home health care, you will read a variety of stories ranging from horrific to heart-warming. Our family has been blessed with wonderful LPNs and RNs who have worked with Verity anywhere from a few months to a few years. As I write this, we have two amazing ladies who have shared the Monday through Friday daytime shifts for over three years. They adore Verity, know her needs, and care for her as well as (or even better than!) her father and I do. Though I was initially hesitant about having a stranger come into our home and care for my fragile baby, we quickly adjusted to life with a nurse once we decided to try having one in our home when Verity turned eight months old. For our family, having a nurse care for Verity during the weekdays allowed me to mother my other children (whom we homeschool) and take care of the basic tasks of household management that had fallen by the wayside when I was in over my head caring for a fragile baby whom we were afraid would pass at any moment.

Now that Verity is older and not so fragile, our nurses are able to focus her daytime activities on therapeutic exercises, helping her develop and reach her highest potential. They take care of her g-tube feedings and medications and even attend school with her since she needs complete care at all times. They do far more than I can adequately describe, and I am grateful beyond words for these ladies who have become like family to us.

At the same time, I recognize that our experience is not universal. Many dear friends have had such terrible experiences with home nursing that they decided it wasn't worth it. These moms and dads give their children 100% of their care 100% of the time. I will not recount any specific stories here, but I do encourage you to research, research, research! Find home health care agencies in your area and do some digging. What do their client families say about their services? Interview different agencies. Find out what services your child qualifies for, and remember YOU are in the driver's seat when it comes to selecting a provider. Ultimately, you have the say over who comes into your home and cares for your child. "Nanny cams" (video monitors) should be a serious consideration if not a given.

At the very least, check out your options—even if you are not comfortable with home health care in the beginning of your journey, you may find that you can use some help in the future. This leads to another possible option that may help your family.

Respite programs/providers

All parents need a break from time to time, and special-needs parents especially so. From taking some time for self-care to having a date night with your spouse, respite care can allow you to be at your best when you are caring for your precious baby. Respite care can be having a trusted family member or friend come over regularly to take care of your baby so you can shower, sleep, or get groceries by yourself. Many special needs families find that a grandmother, aunt, or best friend (or maybe a combination of multiple people who love you!) end up being a win-win situation for everyone: for the family who definitely needs some help as well as for the caregivers who have the privilege of learning how to care for your sweet baby so they can enjoy that special time with him or her.

We have a friend who asked us if she could come over and be trained on how to take care of Verity during the night so that Ted and I could get an uninterrupted night of sleep. At the time, Verity was nine months old, and we hadn't slept more than a couple of hours at a time since before her birth. Edie worked online and had a very flexible schedule. Once she knew how to care for Verity at night, she blessed us by coming over one night a week to give us respite. Now, some years later, she is still coming over as her schedule allows!

If a personal connection isn't an option for you to receive respite care, you may choose to access professional respite providers through community resources. Costs may be covered by a Medicaid waiver or by other means, or you can make private arrangements if your budget allows. As with home health care services, you will have the opportunity to interview any potential caregivers and make sure the company providing respite services meets your needs and expectations. As it turns out, we were able to have our friend Edie jump through hoops to become our official respite provider once Verity was approved for Medicaid services. Edie's gift of serving our family turned into an opportunity for her to earn a little extra income. So think about this as well—perhaps a friend or family member who is already helping you out can become a paid respite provider.

Paid parent programs

A few states recognize the sacrifice parents make when bringing a special-needs child into the family and provide earning opportunities accordingly. Colorado is one of these places.

When we moved here a few months after Verity was born, our early intervention team told us I could become a parent CNA (certified nursing assistant) and get paid for taking care of Verity. While our circumstances did not allow me to investigate this immediately, a year later I went through training and passed the state exam to become a CNA. Our home health care agency then hired me as an additional caregiver for Verity, and we have been blessed to receive paychecks for tasks I would do for my sweet daughter anyway! This has helped our family tremendously. Obviously I am not in a position to work away from our home. The fact that our state understands this kind of situation and is supportive of families who care for these special individuals is something we do not take for granted.

Other family members may be able to be paid caregivers as well, not only parents. Different states have different requirements and opportunities, so be sure to investigate. Some places will require a level of formalized training before a family member is eligible to receive payment for care given.

Some families even choose to move to a different state based on provisions such as this. As you research your options with Medicaid and other community-based programs, this might be something to keep in mind when making long-term decisions.

Supplemental Security Income (SSI)

SSI is a federal program funded by general tax revenues that provides monies for disabled individuals to help provide for their basic needs. For the most up-to-date information, including eligibility requirements and the application process, visit the government website: ssa.gov/ssi

Medical equipment

Depending on your child's needs, you may be sent home from the hospital with medical equipment for supporting your baby. This equipment may be used temporarily or long term. The hospital staff will help you connect with a DME company (durable medical equipment). Often insurance will make payments on a machine for a period of time; if you are still using the machine after it is paid for, the equipment then becomes yours. Clarify with your insurance and the DME company if you have any questions about this process.

Certain machines also require consumable supplies. For example, the fact that Verity receives nutrition via her feeding pump means that our monthly supply order includes feeding bags (a new one each day), a G-tube replacement kit, formula, extension tubes, and gauze and syringes. We don't order every item every month, only as needed. Likewise, we have a respiratory supply company that provides items related to Verity's CPAP and suction machines and pulse oximeter. Our supply companies contact us monthly when it is time to place our order, and we go through the checklist to see what is needed. (It's amazing how quickly this becomes normal! Don't worry—you will learn what you need when you need it.)

Home considerations and modifications

As you think about bringing your baby home from the hospital, give some thought to where he or she will sleep and how you might arrange the additional supplies that come with medical equipment. You may choose to have Baby sleep in your room. Many parents I know do this for an extended time, although you might also need to make arrangements with your spouse to "pass the torch" so you can get some uninterrupted sleep on occasion! (Ted and I often split the night—he would go to bed at 8pm, and I would wake him at 1:00 in the morning, or later if I could stand it, since he had to work the next day.)

Thinking a bit longer term, will your baby move to his or her own bedroom? Verity has remained in an open space in our home. It's her "room," but it would technically be the front office or sitting room in a "normal" house! This allows us to have easy access to her, as we sleep in our bedroom with the door open just a few steps away so we can hear when she has a need or when the machines alarm.

Other considerations: perhaps one day you will want or need a ramp to get in and out of the house or garage. There are also modifications that may be needed for the primary vehicle for transporting your child. Since we live in snowy Colorado, we made sure our next car purchase was a vehicle with all-wheel drive in case we need to take Verity to the hospital in an emergency.

Medicaid and other community programs can help provide for accessibility modifications as well as specialized items, such as a safe bed for sleeping in as your child outgrows a crib.

Caring for an individual with limited mobility will mean adapting and modifying your environment accordingly. Special equipment is available to help with bathing, toileting, and other activities of daily life. These are not necessarily things you have to figure out immediately, and keep in mind you will have help as you navigate each step in your journey.

Family dynamics

As we bring this chapter to a close, let's consider what family life will be like when you bring home a fragile little one. If this is the case for you, it may be that you anticipate only having some days or weeks with your baby. Or perhaps the prognosis is better than expected and you will have months or years.

Do you have other children at home? If so, talk with them about how you would like them to safely engage with their baby brother or sister. Explain the various medical supplies and routines Baby will need once you know what they are yourself. Help them understand what is absolutely off limits—little hands can grab tubes and wires all too quickly! Perhaps you can modify a doll or stuffed animal to mimic some of their sibling's unique qualities—we have a teddy bear with a G-button and a doll modified to look like Verity with some of her adaptive equipment.[1] Even if the siblings are young, don't be afraid to let them touch and be close to their baby brother or sister. They can learn boundaries, and with time and training, they will become tremendous assets as they grow older! I didn't know whether to laugh or cry as I watched my two-year-old run to Verity's supplies and lug the suction machine over to me when Verity was having a vomiting episode. Rhema didn't know what a "normal" baby sister needed, but she absolutely knew how to love and care for

Verity from the start. Now, several years later, she is an amazing big sister who takes great delight in reading to and playing with Verity as well as loudly proclaiming Verity's developmental progress to anyone who will listen.

Consider what your immediate family will need and desire when you bring Baby home. Surely other family members will want to visit as well. This should be encouraged if at all possible. At the same time, your baby may need extra precautions because of health concerns. Do not assume everyone will know what this means. It will be your job to lovingly and gently educate those who come into your home (or even into your "bubble" when you are out and about with Baby). Would you like shoes to come off at the door? Should people wash or sanitize their hands before touching your little one? (Um, yes!) Or maybe you prefer no one touch your baby! Whatever you feel is appropriate consideration for your child, make your wishes known.

We had fairly strict protocols in the beginning, which have become more relaxed as Verity has proven herself to be healthier than the "immune-compromised" child we thought she would be based on her diagnosis alone. At the same time, we know how important it is to be careful, especially during "sick season," and we have protocols in place to keep her healthy and out of the hospital.

Ideas for communicating include signs on your front door or in your child's space and even on the car seat and/or stroller. A few I've seen:

"Please look, don't touch; Mommy thanks you so much!"

"Your germs are too big for me!"

"STOP! Please wash your hands before touching!"

Hopefully your extended family and your community will get on board with whatever your wishes are concerning your special baby. Ongoing communication is helpful, as you receive more information from your medical team and can process and disseminate it to those in your closest circles. Sadly, some families have felt they must isolate from loved ones because those family members do not understand (or refuse to abide by) the guidelines parents set up in order to protect their fragile babies. Don't be afraid to set loving, firm boundaries for your and your baby's sakes.

Chapter 17

Preparing Your Birth Plan

[My son] lived for over just an hour. The time was amazing. We had to fight for the C-section, but I wanted to hold him alive if I could. They said he would be so weak he most likely wouldn't survive a delivery. I'm glad I fought for that. The hospital was incredibly laid back in their language about his life and death and not wasting a C-section on this kind of baby; they would save it for my other babies. It was MY time to have with my son, and I wouldn't change it for a second. I'm glad I fought for it.

–Kitrina

It's time to bring everything together and formulate your birth plan if you haven't already done so. The previous chapters have undoubtedly given you much to think about, and you probably have some strong opinions based on what you've read and learned thus far on your journey. The birth plan will give you the opportunity to put into one document your philosophy of birthing your special baby as well as your specific desires surrounding the experience. Having your preferences written down will help you prioritize and make decisions when things are happening in a whirlwind.

If you have our pregnancy journal, you will find the Birth Plan Brainstorming pages helpful in crafting your final document. If not, no worries—this chapter will give you the opportunity to think through various aspects of labor and delivery. Additionally, if you like, you can download and print a complimentary birth plan worksheet from our nonprofit website, VeritysVillage.com.

Diagnosis and parental understanding thereof

Begin your plan with a brief description of your child's specific diagnosis and any relevant findings known up to this point. If desired, you can give space in this section to sharing your own understanding of your baby's condition and offering your thoughts on what this means to you. This helps frame the document—if you communicate the value you place on your baby's life regardless of the diagnosis, your medical team will understand the importance of your requests for potential interventions to meet your baby alive and support his or her life as well as honor your requests in the event the baby is stillborn. It is helpful for your team to know what your knowledge and expectations are coming into this experience.

Labor and delivery

If you have a choice, do you prefer a vaginal delivery or a C-section? In Kitrina's situation, quoted at the beginning of this chapter, she learned her son would most likely not survive a vaginal delivery. Because she wanted to meet him alive if at all possible, she asked for a C-section and was able to spend time with him before he passed. Some doctors do not willingly perform these operations on mothers when they feel the baby is not likely to live long, so it may be something for which you need to advocate if it is what you desire. Remember, you are allowed to change your mind and switch plans at any time! You may wish to try for a vaginal delivery with measures in place in the event an emergency C-section is needed if Baby is in distress. Or you may choose to schedule a C-section to ensure safety for both Mom and Baby. Your plan can include "if/then" measures with provisions for different circumstances.

How do you feel about induction of labor? Speaking in ***general*** terms, if it is at all possible to allow labor to happen naturally, this is usually preferable for both mother and baby. Induced labor can be much more painful and includes the risk of needing additional interventions. Early induction can contribute to respiratory difficulties for babies. At the same time, if the mother or baby's life is in danger, inducing labor may be the best and safest option for delivery. You will definitely need to have ongoing discussions with your doctor about this issue, and if you agree to an induction, make sure you also agree with the reasons given for why it is necessary.

How long are you willing to go past your due date? I know a mother who delivered her daughter 16 days after she was due! My doctor agreed to let me go at least a week past our due date and then evaluate our situation. I was willing to go even two weeks past, but Verity came sooner.

What are your feelings about pain relief during the labor and delivery process? Do you wish to try for an unmedicated delivery if possible? Or would you prefer an epidural be in place in case an emergency C-section needs to be performed?

Again, all these considerations should be explored and discussed with your medical providers. Even with a plan in place, unforeseen circumstances often necessitate a much different approach, so try to explore all the possibilities. Ask for help and input from other medical professionals as well as other parents within your growing support community.

For additional mental, emotional, and even spiritual support, you might consider reaching out to a doula. Still Birthday has a wonderful network of birth and bereavement doulas who are trained to provide sensitive, client-centered care for these circumstances. Having been through the training myself, I can vouch for the love and compassion with which these doulas approach the birth experience. You will also find many examples of birth plans on the Still Birthday web site.

Approved attendees

Whom would you like in the delivery room with you? Whom will you allow to see you and the baby following birth? Be sure to list the names (or positions) of your support team, such as your spouse, photographer, doula, specific family members, clergy, or other important people in your life. Consider whom you wish to celebrate with in person if your baby is alive…and consider whom you are comfortable having by your side if your baby passes.

After-birth activities

Would you like Baby on your chest immediately after delivery? Along with this, would you like skin-to-skin time if possible? How and when do you prefer evaluations be done? (For example, we asked for as much as possible to be done on my chest, with routine care such as suctioning, toweling off, eye ointment, etc. waiting so we could evaluate her condition and give Baby as much skin-to-skin time as possible.) Some parents ask for delayed cord clamping because of the many benefits of waiting. Others don't mind the clamping of the umbilical cord to happen whenever the delivery team is ready to do so.

What type of breathing support would you like the team to administer if needed? Are there any measures you do NOT want your team to take? Some parents wish for any interventions necessary to help their baby breathe—others are concerned about the effects of CPR or intubation on a fragile baby. Remember it is perfectly all right to ask for something different at delivery than you outlined on your birth plan. Right now you are simply thinking through your options. This is a difficult and burdensome task, so pray for wisdom and trust that you will be guided to do the right thing for your precious baby when the time comes.

Does your baby's diagnosis require special evaluations prior to attempted feedings? What are your desires for giving your baby nutrition? Would you like to establish your breast milk supply, and if so, will you need to ask for a hospital-grade pump? If your baby is unable to nurse, would you like the team to give nutrition via a feeding tube or IV?

Based on what you already know about your baby's condition, what are some other pertinent considerations for delivery and after-care? For example, would you like an echocardiogram to determine the exact condition of the heart after Baby is stabilized? Would a brain scan be appropriate? If you aren't sure what to ask for at this point, check in with your support network and ask experienced parents what they recommend so you can include it in your birth plan.

If Baby is stillborn

Finally…this is not easy to think about, but what would you like to have happen in the event Baby is stillborn? While you don't need to outline every single idea in your birth plan, it's helpful to let your team know some general preferences ahead of time. Look back through the ideas in chapter 15 and decide what is a priority for you and your family if the unthinkable happens.

A sample

What follows is the exact birth plan we created for our daughter Verity. I had never had any kind of written plan for any of our other eight children—but then, we were never faced with such uncertainty with those babies, either. You are welcome to use any of this that may apply to your situation. I pray it will be beneficial to you as you think about creating your own birth plan.

Jacobson Birth Plan

Due date February 25, 2017

Mom: Beverly Irene Jacobson
Baby: Verity Irene Jacobson
Dad: J. Ted Jacobson
Sibs: C, T, A, K, L, Z, S, and R Jacobson
Grandparents: Rhonda; John and Irene K
Pastor: Jon & Jackie M
Photographer: Melissa P
Visitors: Other family and friends will be welcome once approved.

Prenatal Diagnosis: Full Trisomy 18, via amniocentesis at 18 weeks
Prenatal Ultrasound Observations:

- Clenched fists
- Clubbed feet
- Delayed physical growth

We believe Verity is a true gift from God: every moment we have had and will have with her is a blessing. Although we have a realistic view of Verity's diagnosis, we have never stopped praying for her. Additionally, we have done our own research and made contact with other families in recent months. We have learned that FT18, contrary to being "incompatible with life," is instead a condition that, while certainly dealing with special needs and challenges, does not preclude the child or her family from experiencing the joys of life…no matter how short or long that life may be.

We ask that our baby be referred to by her name, Verity.

We would like to find a comfortable balance between interventions to help her live longer and not creating any extra needed pain or discomfort for her. We would like any interventions to be based on vital signs and Verity's specific needs, rather than her diagnosis of Trisomy 18.

It is important to us that no one enters the room during or after delivery without being fully aware of our situation and wishes – this includes family and medical staff.

NOTE: We reserve the right to alter this birth plan at any time!
While we understand circumstances may render our preferences a moot point, the following describes our desires as we think through possibilities.
Labor & Delivery:
Pain Relief: no narcotics - epidural only as I wish to stay alert and aware
Vaginal Delivery: This is preferred. However, we would like Verity monitored during labor, and if she shows continued signs of distress we would like a C-section delivery if it means the difference between delivering her alive instead of stillborn. I would like to tentatively plan on getting an epidural immediately after being admitted since we expect Verity to be small and labor may be short. I will do what is necessary to help stabilize her and deliver her alive. I wish to have my husband and photographer present in the room during labor and delivery.
C-Section Delivery: If a C-section is needed due to fetal distress and could get Verity out alive, we would like to switch to this option. Please keep my pain management to epidural only as I would like to remain alert and aware. I would like my husband and photographer in the room.

At Birth:

- We would like Verity immediately placed on my chest after birth.
- We are ok with immediate resuscitation if needed (CPR, oxygen, etc…) If intubation is the only thing keeping Verity from living, and its effects will be treatable moving forward, meaning her heart is functioning well and nothing else is causing life-threatening concerns, please proceed.
- She is to have delayed cord clamping from the umbilical cord for at least two minutes after the placenta has been passed.
- We would like as much skin-to-skin time as possible.
- Any evaluations that need to be done immediately, we ask for as much as possible be done on my chest. Any routine care (toweling off, eye ointment, vitamin K etc) can wait so we can evaluate Verity's condition and give her as much skin to skin time as possible.
- We would like Verity to be evaluated to determine if there are any esophageal abnormalities before attempting feeds.
- If Verity is able to nurse, we will try to do so. We understand that Verity may need help, and we support interventions that will allow her to receive nourishment in the early hours and days after her arrival if

she is unable to orally feed either through lack of suckling reflex or any esophageal abnormalities.

Post Delivery:
As parents we would like to follow Verity's lead during all interventions to find a balance between helping her live longer and not putting pressure or pain on her body that she can't withstand. *We would like Verity's life supported based on her vital signs and any of her specific defects, NOT based on the Trisomy diagnosis.* We would like all possible resuscitation work on Verity to be done in the delivery room OR near the parents. If Verity has to be taken elsewhere for care, Ted will go with her, and I would like to be taken to her as soon as possible.

We understand that after birth Verity may have more or fewer medical problems than originally anticipated. We ask that all treatment options be discussed with us as parents as you see issues arise. No students or unnecessary staff present, please. Please hold off on all non-life saving tests (weight, measurements, bath, footprints, etc.) until Verity is stabilized. Once stabilized, we would like Verity to receive an ultrasound of her heart and brain to confirm any prenatal defect specifics. We do not approve distress medications, such as morphine, unless further discussed. ***Verity must be accompanied by a parent at all times.***

Potential Medical Care Summary:
__ delivery of oxygen through non-invasive measures (blow-by, nasal cannula)
__ delivery of oxygen through invasive measures (CPAP, Intubation)
__ administration of CPR (chest compressions, ambu bag)
__ administration of resuscitation medications (ex: epinephrine)

Feeding: We would like Verity to be fully evaluated to determine if there are any esophageal abnormalities before attempting feeds. *Aspiration due to low muscle tone is a concern*, and we want to protect her lungs.
__ swallow evaluation
__ IV feedings
__ nasal gastric tube placed; feedings initiated

Post Stabilized Tests:
__ head ultrasound to determine any specific defects/abnormalities
__ cardiac testing to rule out any missed cardiac abnormalities
__ sleep study to check for apnea

For home care:
__ Massimo monitor for Verity's pulse/o2 sats

If Verity is stillborn:
We would like to hold Verity as long as we need, waiting to take any measurements or do any routine procedures. We would like to bathe and dress her and have photographs taken. We would like the opportunity to make hand and footprints and/or molds.

At this point we do not have any information on what happens with Verity should we lose her in the hospital, and we would like to discuss these options with the appropriate party.

Finally, we understand and anticipate that this will be a difficult birth for everyone, including the medical staff providing our care. We greatly appreciate your service and understand we cannot do this without you. Thank you for your commitment to our AND our daughter's care and well-being.

Chapter 18

From Diagnosis to Delivery...and Beyond

Take every day and every obstacle one at a time. If not, you will get burnt out quickly. It's ok to take time for yourself. Mental health matters too.

–Ariel

Oh, Mama. Can I be real with you? I've put off writing this chapter for so long. I'm emotionally invested in this book—emotionally invested in ***you***. I don't know why I've been procrastinating so. I've worked on the format, added more amazing quotes from experienced parents, tweaked the table of contents. And now…now I finally sit down to attempt to share my heart one last time. Is what I've written here enough? Did I address the inevitable questions adequately? Did my reader find hope and help for this journey? Oh, God, may it be so!

Sweet mama, dear father—I have poured out so many prayers on your behalf. I have prayed for your precious baby, praying over whatever time you will get to spend with him or her. And I have prayed for any children you have now or may have in the future. I pray for the legacy and testimony being written even now, a beautiful story with an eternal purpose. May peace and blessings wash over your heart as you consider how very, very loved you are!

At the beginning of our time together, we talked about the goals for this book. My prayer is that you have *centered yourself* so you can think and act in ***alignment*** with your values and worldview. Second, I hope you have a driving desire to *educate yourself* so you can have ***assurance*** that you are making the best decisions for your baby and your family. And third, I hope you are ready to *prepare yourself* as much as is possible on a journey of this nature so you can find ***significance*** in your experience, knowing there is meaning and purpose no matter what happens.

Here's the thing: no matter how this journey "ends" for you, it's not really the end. If your baby is born alive, if you bring that precious bundle home despite the odds, you are still forging new ground, learning how to care for a unique child with needs that may be far different from anything you've encountered before. Your journey as a special-needs parent will take off as you grow into your new role. However long you have with your child here on earth, this little human will continually change and shape you. (This is true of all of our children, I know—and yet somehow even more so for one whose life expectancy is limited.)

And if your baby is stillborn or passes before long, even that is not the end of this journey. You will always be that child's parent, and while you may find the pain of loss changing over time, the experience will be woven into your very identity, something you will carry with you until you meet eternity yourself.

No one ever really asks for this. During my pregnancy with Verity, I often felt like little Frodo on the way to Mordor with the ring of power, telling Gandalf in despair, "I wish the ring had never come to me. I wish none of this had happened!"

If you are a fan of the Lord of the Rings series, perhaps you recall Gandalf's reply: "So do all who live to see such times. But that is not for them to decide. All we have to decide is what to do with the time that is given to us."

While I hope this book has given you much in the way of practical ideas and suggestions to consider as you decide what to do with the time that is given to you…I also pray your heart is being stirred even beyond that. Do you view your child's life story as a gift or a burden? Right now this whole situation may feel like a burden too big to see beyond. But I promise you, if you allow it to happen, your perspective will shift. As you mentally adjust to your new normal, as you work through shifting emotions, you will emerge into a more spacious place, a place free from the bondage of fear and doubt.[1]

As difficult as it may be to see right now, this situation in which you have been unceremoniously plunked affords you a most profound opportunity. Whether you asked for it or not, you now have the potential to effect change in many lives, starting with your own. Will you inspire positive change in your marriage? In your family? In your community? In the medical world? Who else might be blessed and encouraged because of what you are going through now?

Perhaps you're not ready to think beyond this moment, and that's all right. I know I certainly wasn't able to focus much beyond getting through each moment and processing whatever tidbit I had learned that day. And yet, with the benefit of some years of hindsight, I can honestly say how very glad, how thankful I am that God put Verity in our family! I'm thankful He allowed me to go through those moments of fear and agonizing anxiety. Truly, I'm thankful for every bit of this journey, even the hard parts, even the parts I'm ashamed of, because all of it—every single bit—has changed me and made me more like Jesus…Jesus, my Lord and Savior, who endured the cross, despising its shame.[2]

During my pregnancy and the early months with Verity, I never would have imagined starting a nonprofit supporting other families who receive a life-limiting diagnosis. I never would have imagined writing books and resources to help others on a similar journey. I never would have imagined the friends I'd make from all over the world, laughing and crying with them and sharing our hearts in a way only those of us who have been on this road would understand.

What's in store for you? I know your mind is consumed these days with wondering what is in store for your sweet baby. But what about ***you***? Where might this journey take you personally? You don't have to know the answer to that right now. Simply decide in your heart that you will allow this time that has been given to you to count for something greater than yourself.

Then, from diagnosis to delivery and beyond, you will find yourself part of a story far greater than you could ever have imagined.

A blessing for you

The Lord bless you and keep you;
the Lord make his face to shine upon you and be gracious to you;
the Lord lift up his countenance upon you and give you peace.[3]

Now may the Lord of peace himself give you peace at all times in every way. The Lord be with you all.[4]

APPENDIX A

My Foundation of Faith

Each worldview must address some basic questions. While we could ask many questions to get to the heart of my belief system, in this brief appendix I will address three: *Who am I? What's wrong with the world? How can it be fixed?*

Here I share the answers to which much prayer and study have led my husband and myself, along with many others who believe the Bible to be the inspired word of God. If your answers to these questions are different, ask yourself why. Don't be afraid to challenge your own beliefs. Truth can withstand questioning. As Hebrews 11:6 says, "And without faith it is impossible to please him, for whoever would draw near to God must believe that he exists and that he rewards those who seek him."

Are you earnestly seeking God? Do you seek truth? Ask for truth to be revealed to you, to either confirm what you already believe or to make you restless and dissatisfied until you know that you know that you KNOW the truth. For the truth, my friend, will set you FREE!

Who am I?

According to Genesis 1 and 2, I am a human being created in the image of God. As such, I am different from the animals, set apart for God's holy purposes, and given charge to steward and care for the earth and its resources. As a woman, I am different from (not less than) my husband, because male and female display different yet complementary characteristics of the same creator.

According to Genesis 3 and various passages in the letter to the Romans, I am a sinner. I knew right and chose wrong; I knew wrong and chose it anyway. On my own, I could not bridge the gap between myself and a perfect, holy God who cannot be in the presence of sin.

And yet! As I read the whole story of mankind set forth in Scripture, I see the lovingkindness of God the Father, who knew His created beings could not overcome sin. In His mercy and grace, He sent Jesus, the radiance of God's glory and the exact imprint of His nature (Hebrews 11:3), to earth. Jesus lived on earth, fully God and fully man, and because of His sinless nature, when He died on the cross, it was as the perfect sacrifice required to atone for sin. He took my place—He bore my punishment. Because I have accepted this arrangement, because I believe Jesus not only died in my place but also rose from the grave three days later, I have a new position. I am no longer on death row, waiting to be punished for my wrongdoing. I am free, and I am alive in Christ—not only here on earth, but forevermore as I will be in heaven when my earthly body passes away.

What's wrong with the world?

Clearly we see this is a broken world with much pain and suffering. The fact you are reading this book is proof of that—babies are not always born healthy, and in fact, sometimes babies die. In fact, many seemingly good people die before their time. War, famine, disease, injustice, and unbearable hardships are a fact of life. Why? If there is a God, why all this suffering?

In the answer to the previous question, I admitted that I am by nature a sinner. This, in fact, is the case for every human being who has ever lived (aside from Jesus, but he was 100% human and 100% God, which clearly is not the case for any other human being). Because sin is present—even prevalent—in the world, we live with horrific, horrendous effects of that sin. We tend to think of wrongdoing as only affecting the human realm, but the truth is every bad thing on earth is a result of sin. Sickness, famine, acts of nature that destroy lives—those too are a result of living in a fallen world. And of course much suffering happens because human beings hurt others on both a small and large scale.

Couldn't God remove all these effects of sin? Couldn't He hold back the hurricanes? Provide relief from a pandemic? Stop those whose choices are harming others and causing the most pain? Well, there's the rub. *Choice.* We all have the freedom to choose, don't we? The problem comes when our choices interfere with other people living their lives. God's sovereignty still allows for people to choose their own path, which may or may not take His wise ways into account.

How can the world be fixed?

As an individual, I have received God's "fix" for my sin: salvation through Jesus Christ. All those who have received this free gift are part of what we call the "Body of Christ," or the Church (big-C Church, not just your local church building). When people who follow Jesus allow Him to continue working change in their lives, purifying and refining them (because we still struggle with sin, even though we are set free from its eternal effects), then God's power and compassion are unleashed on earth. Christians are the vessels through which God helps and heals some of the brokenness of this world.

But there's still so much suffering, you say. Yes, it's true. Yet this isn't the end of the story. We know we were made for eternity—the Bible tells us God has set eternity in all of our hearts. Whether we realize it or not, we yearn for something beyond this world. We were created to love and worship God, not ourselves. While God chooses to work on earth through and among His people, He is also preparing for the day when He will right every wrong. He will pay retribution to those who persist in pride and selfishness, refusing to acknowledge Him as Lord. And He will make all things new, ushering in a new heaven and a new earth, prepared for those who have accepted Him as King and Savior.

APPENDIX B

OF HEALING AND MIRACLES

Written on Verity's blog November 8, 2016

I'm learning that faith in the fire isn't easily defined. We can say we believe something, have Scripture to prove our points, and then find ourselves being tossed by the waves of circumstances beyond our previous realm of experience. All we can do is keep our heads above water, gulp enough air for breathing, and trust that the faith nurtured by the Holy Spirit is enough to keep us buoyant until the seas grow calm.

The "air" I'm inhaling, then, is the truth I KNOW, the foundation I don't even have to think about.

God is real.

God is love.

God is all-powerful.

God is eternal and ever-present.

Let's add a life vest—other truths that are buckled tightly around me and keep me from flailing and slipping underwater when I grow weary.

God has saved me through Jesus Christ and will never let me go.

God is sovereign; God is good; God has eternal purposes beyond what I can see.

God's ways are higher than my ways, His thoughts higher than my thoughts.

This part is easy. These things I know. What I do NOT know is how, exactly, God will wield His power and work His purposes in particular situations.

God is all-powerful: so can God do miracles? Of course—Jesus used miracles to prove His claim that He is the Son of God.

God is eternal: so does He do miracles in these days when Jesus Christ doesn't walk in a physical body on earth? Undoubtedly—many of us can testify to supernatural works that can only be attributed to the intervening hand of the Lord.

God is sovereign: so does God bring healing that overrides a doctor's diagnosis? Sure, sometimes…I don't have proof of this, but I suspect God really gets a kick out of showing up and showing off when people predict doom and gloom. I think He takes delight in doing the unexpected in order to get someone's attention and draw them to Himself. (Come on…a donkey speaking to Balaam? A boy defeating a giant with a slingshot? A Jewish girl chosen as queen of Persia who just happens to save her people from mass slaughter? I could go on...)

So yes, I know these things. I believe God is powerful. I believe that if He wanted to, God could "heal" Verity.

Let me tell you what I don't know. I don't know what to say—how to respond—to kindhearted, well-meaning, faith-filled, encouraging proclamations about how people are praying for healing for Baby Verity, praying for nothing less than a miracle.

The night we got confirmation that Verity has full Trisomy 18 (as opposed to partial or "mosaic" T18), we talked with our older four kids about what all this means. Our 13-year-old son asked if God could heal Verity—heal her in the sense of making her "normal."

I answered carefully. "CAN God heal her? Of course. He COULD. He is able. But in order to make her NOT have this condition, He would have to reverse what He has already set in motion. Verity has an extra 18th chromosome *in every single cell of her body*, and unless He chooses to intervene in miraculous ways, that extra chromosome is always going to be there."

What I didn't want then (or now, truthfully)? False hope. A hope that rests on Verity somehow becoming "normal," all because we hope and pray for healing and wait expectantly for a miracle. And so that night, I gently squashed the idea of praying for Verity's healing, mostly because I myself feel that God's purposes for Verity's life are not of the miraculous, physical-healing kind.

I will say, however…after a few weeks of wrestling over various thoughts and emotions, God gently showed me that He WILL bring healing for Verity—she will be healed and made whole in heaven, if not here on earth. And so I had another talk with our family, this time telling them that I was sorry if I had discouraged them from praying healing prayers for their baby sister. I still think that "healing" can mean different things to different people, and I still emphasize that heaven is our real home, and THAT is where all things will be restored and renewed. So our prayers for healing WILL be answered, ultimately. And if they keep these things in mind…if they aren't expecting a "healing" or a "miracle" to look a certain way…if they are open to God's answer being perfect, no matter what it looks like…then, children—friends—by all means, pray for healing!

Am I wrong to put these mental limits, all these caveats, on our prayers—especially the prayers of other people?

It's an honest question.

If someone feels led to pray for Verity's full, restorative healing—who am I to stop that? Pray. Pray as you feel led. But I need to share where God has led ME, and that is to a peace that whatever happens, God has ALREADY done miracles. (Verity is already knit together and growing in my womb, fearfully and wonderfully made, *just as she is*.) God has ALREADY answered prayers. And I fully expect that He will continue to answer prayers and do miracles.

But…my miracle may not be as glorious as you envision.

My miracle may be bravely enduring labor knowing I will give birth to a stillborn baby.

My miracle may be that I have strength each day to care for a special-needs child with love and compassion, a thought that both drains and terrifies me.

My miracle may be losing our girl to the arms of Jesus just as we have finally learned to "do life" with her and all her needs, nurses, and equipment.

My miracle may be praising God and embracing the life He has given me when I would rather curl up and die.

You know what? On second thought…pray for miracles. Please…pray for miracles.

NOTES

Chapter 1: How to Move Past an Unexpected Diagnosis

1. 1 John 4:19
2. Matthew 10:29-31
3. Psalm 139:13, 16
4. John 10:28
5. 2 Samuel 13:23

Chapter 5: Dealing with Emotions

1. Patricia Smith, "You Are Not Alone," Center for Parent Information & Resources, January 2014, parentcenterhub.org/notalone/
2. Matthew 6:34, NIV
3. You may find the pregnancy journal I created for mamas with a prenatal diagnosis helpful. If you don't already have one, you can find it here: store.vervante.com/c/v/V4081903377-01
4. 2 Corinthians 1:3-4

Chapter 6: Living with Uncertainty

1. Stanford University, "Living with uncertainty: How to accept and be more comfortable with unpredictability," Stanford Today, November 4, 2020, news.stanford.edu/today/2020/11/04/living-with-uncertainty/
2. Verity's Village (veritysvillage.com), Abel Speaks (abelspeaks.org), and Be Not Afraid (benotafraid.net) are all faith-based organizations that support families who receive a life-limiting diagnosis.

Chapter 7: Unpacking Preconceived Ideas

1. Denis Cavanaugh et al., "Changing Attitudes of American Ob/Gyns on Legal Abortion," *Female Patient* 20 (May 1995).
2. Bridget Mora, "Prenatal Testing and the Denial of Care," *Ethics & Medics*, 43.2 (February 2018).

3. Heidi Faith, "I Am a DOLIU M0M," Still Birthday, July 28, 2014, stillbirthday.com/2014/07/doliu-m0m/

Chapter 8: What Does Current Research Say?

1. Planned Parenthood, "Personal Stories: How Bans on Abortion Later in Pregnancy Hurt People," *Planned Parenthood Action Fund*, accessed January 8, 2021, www.plannedparenthoodaction.org/issues/abortion/20-week-bans/personal-stories-reveal-how-20-week-abortion-bans-would-hurt-wom
2. John Hopkins All Children Hospital, "Center for Congenital Diaphragmatic Hernia," accessed January 8, 2021, hopkinsallchildrens.org/Services/Pediatric-General-Surgery/Conditions/Congenital-Diaphragmatic-Hernia

Chapter 9: What If…?

1. Janvier A, Farlow B, Barrington KJ. 2016. Parental hopes, interventions, and survival of neonates with trisomy 13 and trisomy 18. Am J Med Genet Part C Semin Med Genet 999C:1-9.
2. Ibid.
3. Ibid.
4. Bridget Mora, "Prenatal Testing and the Denial of Care," *Ethics & Medics*, 43.2 (February 2018).

Chapter 10: What Does Your Medical Team Say?

1. Viki Kind, "What is the difference between palliative care, comfort care and hospice care?" *KindEthics.com,* June 29, 2009. kindethics.com/2009/06/what-is-the-difference-between-palliative-care-comfort-care-and-hospice-care/
2. Janvier A, Farlow B, Barrington KJ. 2016. Parental hopes, interventions, and survival of neonates with trisomy 13 and trisomy 18. Am J Med Genet Part C Semin Med Genet 999C:1-9.

Chapter 11: What Do Real People Say?

1. facebook.com/groups/diagnosistodelivery

Chapter 12: What Do YOU Say?

1. Got Questions, "What does it mean to believe in the sanctity of life?" accessed June 26, 2021, gotquestions.org/sanctity-of-life.html
2. Abel Speaks (abelspeaks.org), Be Not Afraid (benotafraid.net), and Verity's Village (veritysvillage.com) are all such organizations.

Chapter 15: Preparing for Loss

1. Our family chose, for example, not to use the word "sick" when we talked about Verity. A Trisomy 18 diagnosis by itself does not mean a person is ill. A genetic condition is different from a sickness or a disease. However, we have met other families who use different terminology so as to help young children come to terms with the possibility of loss. Additionally, sometimes it is easier to explain a complex diagnosis in more simplistic terms to strangers in passing conversation. Consider WHAT you desire to communicate, and then you can choose HOW to communicate it.
2. Our book *Our Baby Will Be Different* is available in both a girl version and a boy version through Amazon. Though the text was written with a few common Trisomy 18 characteristics in mind (hands, feet, brain/ developmental delays), families facing other diagnoses have found it helpful as well. The book is written from a biblical understanding of the value of all human life and ends on a hopeful note—no matter what happens on earth, in heaven our baby will be different!
3. To purchase the NICU journal on Amazon: https://amzn.to/2SKgaTJ

Chapter 16: Preparing for Life

1. The modified Verity doll is a precious gift made possible by donations to my friend Rose Watson's home business. Rose is the mother of Verity's friend Lavender and one of the most talented and creative souls ever. To learn more or order, reach out to her on Instagram @little.miss.seamstress.

Chapter 18: From Diagnosis to Delivery…and Beyond

1. From Psalm 18:19, NIV: "He brought me out into a spacious place; he rescued me because he delighted in me."
2. Hebrews 12:2
3. Numbers 6:24-26
4. 2 Thessalonians 3:16

ACKNOWLEDGMENTS

This work, this labor of love, would not have moved from idea to paper if it were not for the encouragement and support of many wonderful people.

First and foremost, my husband: Ted, you have always graciously served your family, me most of all. Thank you for picking up the extra slack when my eyes were glazed over and I was too deep in thought to answer basic questions such as "Should I start dinner?!" I love you always and forever. You bless me so!

To my young adult and teenage "kids:" Thank you for cooking meals and herding younger ones so I could "just finish this one paragraph." You are truly amazing humans, and I am blessed you call me Mom.

To my younger kids: thank you for letting me work so much these last few months. Granted, you got more snacks, chicken nuggets, and computer games than you would have if I hadn't been so distracted, but still. I'll love you forever and like you for always. As long as I'm living, my babies you'll be!

To our dear nurses and friends, Yvette and Janet: thank you for letting me think out loud with you about this project. Your encouragement and input is more valuable than I can describe.

To the many moms and dads in online support groups whom I've met over the years since we received Verity's diagnosis: thank you for willingly sharing your wisdom and experience. This book would not be the rich resource it is if it weren't for your willingness to allow your thoughts to be quoted.

And last, but most certainly not least, to the amazing, brave mamas who have brought the From Diagnosis to Delivery support group to life: thank you for joining our community. Thank you for your willingness to be vulnerable and to keep sharing even when it hurts. You inspire me daily. May this work bless and encourage future FD2D members.

Beverly Jacobson is wife to a retired Air Force officer and homeschooling mother of nine children on earth. With two babies in heaven plus a daughter who has Edwards syndrome (Trisomy 18), she is well acquainted with grief and uncertainty. Beverly is the founder and CEO of Verity's Village,

a nonprofit ministry serving families who receive a life-limiting diagnosis for their babies. She is the host of Trisomy Talks, a monthly parent discussion about needs within the rare trisomy community. She has authored several books supporting families who have children with special needs, including *Our Baby Will Be Different* and *UN-Planning Our Parenthood*. She leads the *From Diagnosis to Delivery* online support group, serves in women's ministry in her local church, and loves going out for coffee and one-on-one conversation. Reach out to her at BeverlyJacobson.com.

Verity's Village, inspired by our journey with our daughter Verity Irene, is a community dedicated to providing hope, encouragement, education, and practical support for families who receive a life-limiting diagnosis for their babies. Our vision is to change the narrative surrounding genetic anomalies from heartache to hope. For more information, see VeritysVillage.com.

Made in the USA
Columbia, SC
08 October 2021

46488967R00102